The Bible Answers Senior Adults Questions

THE
BIBLE
ANSWERS
SENIOR
ADULTS
QUESTIONS

Elmer L. Gray

BROADMAN PRESS

NASHVILLE, TENNESSEE

Unless otherwise stated, all Scripture quotations are from the *King James Version* of the Bible.
All Scripture quotations marked NIV are from the Holy Bible, *New International Version*, copyright © 1973, 1978, 1984 by International Bible Society.
All Scripture quotations marked RSV are from the *Revised Standard Version of the Bible,* copyrighted 1946, 1952, © 1971, 1973.

Library of Congress Cataloging-in-Publication Data

Gray, Elmer L.
  The Bible answers senior adults' questions/Elmer L. Gray.
  p. cm.
  ISBN: 0-8054-6028-4
  1. Aged--Religious life. 2. Aged in the Bible. 3. Bible-
  -Miscellanea. I. Title
  BV4580.073 1991
  248.8"5--dc2

                                                         90-35511
                                                            CIP

As a senior adult,
I dedicate this book to our grandchildren
Aliesha Gray Kingsman
Megan and Joshua Gray
Petra and Abraham Jasso

Contents

Should we plan our funeral services in advance?

What will our bodies be like in heaven?
When will the final judgment be and what will it be like?
Is there anything to reincarnation?
Will we know each other in heaven?
Will persons in heaven be sexless?
What is the second coming of Christ and when will it happen?
How can you be ready for the final judgment?
Is heaven as wonderful as they say?

To the Readers

Hi, Senior Adults,

I look forward to meeting you some day at a conference or at the big get-together in heaven.

By the way, when you get to heaven, look for me at the coffee table. I said that at a church and a lady who is older than I am scolded me. She said, "Brother Gray, there won't be any coffee in heaven. We won't want it; we will have Jesus."

I hugged her and answered, "How true! How true!" So, don't look for me at a coffee table. Look for me in the crowd around Jesus.

I hope you like this book. I wrote it with you in mind and I enjoyed writing it. I hope it will disturb you some. Maybe it will give you something to think about.

Most of the questions in the book came from senior adults. Some came from workers with senior adults and some from relatives of senior adults.

Read this book for a daily devotional. You could read a few pages a day for two or three months. It has quite a bit in it to digest in just one reading.

I love you.

1.
Wonderful Words of Life

In Sunday School a little boy mentioned that his grandmother read her Bible a lot. The teacher asked why she did. The boy, who had watched a sister in high school study for exams, said, "I think Grandmother is cramming for the finals."

People of all ages find the Bible worth reading and studying. However, senior adults have more incentive to read the Bible because they know that they will soon meet the Bible's Author.

Senior adults like to read the Bible because they already treasure it. Some of them who grew up reading the *King James Version* do not like the other translations. I can understand that. To me, the *King James Version* sounds like the Bible. My first modern translation was a New Testament translated by Helen Barrett Montgomery. I have a dozen or more modern translations, but the *King James Version* is still my favorite. Among the modern translations, I like the *New International Version* (NIV) best. For years my favorite modern translation was the *Good News Bible* (GNB), and I still like it.

The Bible includes material that will help people of any age. Let's look at what the Bible has especially for persons in their older years.

Senior adults read the Bible for comfort and inspiration. The Bible comforts them in their physical suffering and also in their emotional stress from loneliness and fear. It inspires them to trust more in the presence, power, and love of God. It also inspires them to share their faith and to help others.

The Bible is basically an inspired witness of how God has related to human beings throughout time and of what He plans for them in the future, especially in eternity. It was not written as a book of answers to questions but it does give guidance for all basic human needs.

As you read the questions in this book, you will find that the answers include Scriptures which may refer either directly or indirectly to the questions. If you disagree with the answers, use the Bible and construct your own answers. Seek advice from your pastor or someone who relates to senior adults. Have your answers emphasize what the Bible says about the righteousness, love, and purpose of God. Also major on what the Bible says about the faith we are to have in Jesus Christ as our Lord, the love we are to have for each other, and the hope we are to hold about eternal life and the return of Christ.

A senior adult whose Bible was getting ragged said to a friend, "It looks like my Bible and I are both falling apart."

The friend smiled and answered, "You are certainly not falling apart. The fact that your Bible is falling apart may be what is holding you together."

Where can senior adults find answers for their questions?

In the fall of 1935 I preached my first sermon at a "county poor farm." A dozen old men and women lived there. Most of them were sick or crippled. Back then old people lived either with kids or in places with minimum facilities provided by communities or else they did the best they could for themselves.

In the past hundred years life became more complex and needs increased. Caring for the elderly became a bigger problem.

Now many offer assistance to the rapidly growing senior-adult segment of the population. Specialists help in various ways:

1. Emotional counseling for loneliness and depression;

2. Guiding social relationships in the family and with others;

3. Physical caring for those with diseases of the aged;

4. Financial guidance both in budgeting and in investment;

5. Political rallying of support for senior adult interests;

6. Providing for senior adult recreation and fellowship;

7. Offering many other services.

Most of these efforts are good. However one special need exceeds all of these. That is for senior adults to find God's help along with all of the other good help available.

Does the Lord have help for us on illness, loneliness, hopes, potentials, and other needs? Let's face that question. We shall focus the Bible on the needs of senior adults. Jesus said, "Seek ye first the kingdom of God, and his righteousness; and all these things shall be added unto you"(Matt. 6:33).

Ask God to guide you to find help in His Word.

What can senior adults do when they hurt and are worried?

A man said to a doctor, "When I lift my arm, my chest hurts." The doctor frowned and said, "Don't lift your arm then."

Not all problems are that simple. However, some make problems more complicated than they need to be.

"Hurt" means either to cause or to experience pain and refers basically to physical suffering. "Worry" is being anxious or uneasy. Whether you hurt or worry, you need to do something about the matter. To the best of your ability, identify the problem. Will it take care of itself in time? Is the problem one that you can do something about? Do not let any need go without attention. You are responsible to God for your body, mind, and feelings. As a living soul that must answer to God, you need to take care of the various aspects of your being.

The Bible encourages both physical discipline and medical care. Hurting or worrying, do what you can for yourself, seek and accept help, read God's Word, and do His will. Jesus said, "Come unto me, all ye that labour and are heavy laden, and I will give you rest" (Matt. 11:28).

Remember Paul had his own physician, Luke. Paul spoke highly of both the human body and the human spirit:

> What? know ye not that your body is the temple
> of the Holy Ghost which is in you, which ye have of
> God, and ye are not your own? For ye are bought
> with a price: therefore glorify God in your body,
> and in your spirit, which are God's (1 Cor. 6:19-20).

Ask God to help you take good care of yourself for
His glory.

Can senior adults find meaning in their dreams?

Some senior adults dream more than before and
some less. The scholars say everyone dreams but some
do not remember dreaming.

Dreams are the working of your mind when you do
not deliberately control it. They seem real and arouse
emotional responses ranging from terror to joy. Theories differ about whether dreams mean anything and,
if so, what? People in ancient times took their dreams
as seriously as the experiences they had when awake.
Sigmund Freud, a pioneer in psychoanalysis, looked on
dreams as a way of discovering a person's real desires.

God communicated with some people in their
dreams. The Bible tells that God spoke in the past in
many ways but finally He spoke most clearly through
His Son, Jesus Christ (Heb. 1:1-2). God used many
channels of communication. He even spoke through a
donkey to one prophet (Num. 22:27-31), but that does
not mean for us to rely on donkeys for advice. Nor are
we to rely on the stars, witches, fortune-tellers,
dreams, or anything else other than God's own Son
who is our Lord Jesus Christ. Test all of your own ideas
and those of others with the Bible.

The real question is not whether dreams have meaning but does anything have meaning? Yes, there is meaning. John wrote to that idea in his Gospel: "In the beginning was the Word, and the Word with with God, and the Word was God" (John 1:1).

Ask God to speak to you through His written Word, the Bible, and His Living Word, Jesus Christ, His Son.

Does the Bible explain why there is suffering?

Suffering is real. Everyone suffers and some suffer beyond bearing. Why didn't God create a paradise where we would be happy and praise Him? Come to think of it, that is how He started.

The problem of suffering makes us wonder about the nature of God and the mystery of His own suffering because of our sins.

In a study of the Bible we find six major explanations for suffering.

1. *Punishment.* Suffering is punishment for sin but not all suffering is the direct result of sin (2 Cor. 5:10).

2. *Discipline.* Suffering motivates us to obey the law (Ps. 94:12).

3. *Testing.* Suffering tests us so we rejoice in the victory we win (Hab. 3:18).

4. *Revelation.* Suffering can reveal truth to us (John 6:68).

5. *Sacrifice for others.* Following the example of Christ who suffered to redeem us (John 1:29), we may suffer in order to do good for someone else.

6. *Stimulus to hope.* Suffering can develop patience and comfort which will strengthen hope (Rom. 15:4).

In creating us with free will and saving us, God opened Himself to the suffering described in John 3:16: "For God so loved the world, that he gave his only begotten Son, that whosoever believeth in him, should not perish, but have everlasting life."

Ask God to deliver you from suffering or to give you strength to make your suffering a blessing to others and a glory to God.

Can the Bible give us assurance about the life to come?

I looked out across the Pacific Ocean and saw the horizon, the edge of the world. Soon the sun would set but it would rise on the other side of the world. Land is there and people live there.

Heaven is a reality. Jesus Christ is our assurance of that. Before He died, He said,

> In my Father's house are many mansions: if it were not so, I would have told you. I go to prepare a place for you. And if I go and prepare a place for you, I will come again and receive you unto myself; that where I am, there ye may be also (John 14:2-3).

A disciple asked about the way. "Jesus saith unto him, I am the way, the truth, and the life: no man cometh unto the Father, but by me" (John 14:6).

Paul wrote, "I know whom I have believed, and am persuaded that he is able to keep that which I have committed unto him against that day" (2 Tim. 1:12).

John wrote: "We know that we have passed from death unto life, because we love the brethren" (1 John 3:14).

Job assured us: "I know that my redeemer liveth" (Job 19:25).

Look to the Holy Spirit for assurance. "The Spirit itself beareth witness with our spirit, that we are the children of God" (Rom. 8:16).

One purpose of the Bible is to give us assurance. "These things have I written unto you that believe on the name of the Son of God; that ye may know that ye have eternal life, and that ye may believe on the name of the Son of God" (1 John 5:13).

Ask God to increase your faith and also your love.

What does the Bible mean by Son of God and Son of man?

In Jesus' day people called Him the Son of God and the Son of man. These two terms seem to contradict each other. Most Christians today believe that Christ is the eternal Son of God and that He came in human, fleshly form as Jesus, conceived of the Holy Spirit and born of the virgin Mary.

"Son of God" and "Son of man" seem contradictory today but they did not seem so to people in Jesus' time.

"Son of God" describes the unique relationship Jesus had to God (see John 3:16; 10:30). Christ seldom used the full title "Son of God," but He often referred to God as "my Father" and to Himself as "the Son" when He talked about His relationship to God. "Son of God" fits John's declaration that Christ is coeternal, coequal, and coexistent with God (John 1:1).

Jesus Himself used "Son of man" most. It was an Old Testament term (see Ps. 8; Ezek. 2:1ff; and Dan. 7:13). Scholars differ about what it meant, but by Jesus' time many thought "Son of man" referred to the Messiah, the Coming One. Some say Jesus used it because it did not imply military conquest and political control. Christ Jesus is of God but He is also of us. He is God's

Beloved Son and also our Beloved Lord.

Since Jesus Christ is divine and human, He rightfully took liability for every human being and paid for their violation and damages. Furthermore, He is the Lord who understands the needs of every human being. That is what the dual sonship means.

Thank God for His power and wisdom and for His love and mercy.

What comfort and help does the Bible offer senior adults?

One preacher says his job is to comfort the troubled and to trouble comfortable church members. Comforting someone can range from giving a pillow to sit on to offering a shoulder to cry on.

Our Lord is a God of comfort. Oppression and terror added to the suffering of God's people who felt guilty for their own sins. They found no consolation. The Lord told His great prophet to comfort them: "Comfort, comfort my people, says your God. Speak tenderly to Jerusalem" (Isa. 40:1-2, NIV).

When a hostile takeover disturbed the church at Corinth, Paul wrote to comfort the people. In 2 Corinthians, he used *comfort* eighteen times and the word appears ten times in 2 Corinthians 1:3-7. The God of comfort comforts us so that we might comfort others. Paul also said that the comfort which we have in Christ overflows.

Whether your discomfort is from physical pain, bereavement, financial need, or rejection by people, you will be comforted if you will seek help from God. Here are some ways to find comfort:

1. Read the Bible with an awareness of the Holy Spirit's help.

2. Pray with trust in and love for God.

3. Attend Bible study and worship service regularly.

4. Make friends and enjoy their friendship.

5. If your sorrow and depression continue, seek the help of those who are trained to give such help.

Ask God to comfort you through the love of Christ and His followers.

2.
Amazing Grace

In 1900 the average life expectancy in the United States was about forty-eight years. Half of the babies born that year would not live to be fifty years of age. Things have changed. The average life expectancy climbed over seventy in the 1980s and will almost reach seventy-five by 2000. Half of the babies born this year will live at least until they are seventy.

More people are living to become old. Just what is old age? The public says a professional athlete is old when he is thirty-five or forty. Most people think of retirement as the gate to old age. However, some sixty-five-year-old retirees are younger than some young adults of thirty. In general we measure age by years, but you can't tell a person's age by the number of birthdays he has celebrated.

What does it mean to be a senior adult? "Old age" has its problems and also its benefits. When I was a young preacher, I dared to announce that I would preach next Sunday on how not to grow old. My mother, who lived with us, said she could tell me how not to grow old. Raising my eyebrows, I asked, "How?" She snickered, "Die young."

Frequently someone says, "I don't mind getting old

when I consider the alternative." One person added to that, "I had rather be over the hill than under it."

The situation of senior adults has changed greatly in the past one hundred years. In the early 1900s senior adults lived with younger members of the family or in places sometimes called county poor farms. Many were victims of society. With the increase of social awareness and concern, society made some provision for the elderly.

Once many feared the prospect of becoming poor and old. Now many are comfortable in their advanced years and a number even fare as well or better than in their time of full employment.

Living as a senior adult is enjoyable to many. A man said, "When I retired, I stopped making a living and started making a life." However many senior adults cannot adjust to living without working. A business woman asked frankly, "What's so great about retirement?" Then she added, "I like my work and I'll never retire."

Retirement sounds good to many until they wake up without work to go to and nothing to do all day. Married couples face some of their most difficult days in retirement. Wives have almost shot their retired husbands who tried to teach them efficiency. Husbands have almost left home when their wives tried to harness them to some household tasks.

Hopefully senior adults will become more aware of their needs and problems, their potentials and opportunities, and the enjoyment they can experience and the good they can do. Furthermore, senior adult years are a choice time in which to serve and please the Lord.

When is a person old?

A seventy-year-old speaker said, "When I was sixty, I thought people were young who were fifty. Now I look on anybody under sixty as young."

Old age is not a matter of years. It is more an attitude. Of course a person passes dividing points as he enters different stages of his life.

Through Social Security regulations for retirement, the federal government arbitrarily drew the line at sixty-five. Most people now think that year marks the beginning of old age.

Business affects people's ideas about old age. The job market starts closing to persons as they approach fifty. This reflects an attitude of employers rather than the inability of the fifty-year-old worker. Some organizations have contributed to the concept that fifty is a major dividing line in age by setting that as the minimum age for their members.

The Bible does not establish a certain number of years as the definition of old age. It identifies old age more by appearance and physical ability. A wise man said, "The glory of young men is their strength: and the beauty of old men is the gray head" (Prov. 20:29). Jesus said to Simon Peter, "When thou shalt be old, thou shalt stretch forth thy hands, and another shall gird thee, and carry thee whither thou wouldest not" (John 21:18). To me that says that old age is more a matter of how you look and act. That ancient concept is still good.

Pray that you will look and act the way the Lord wants.

When should a person retire?

If I had known how good retirement was, I would have retired at twenty. Someone heard me say that and said, "How would you have lived?" That's a good question. I couldn't have survived.

Seriously, when should you retire? If you have something you want to do, retire as early as possible. A friend told me, "You shouldn't retire from, you should retire to." If you are not retiring in order to do something, don't retire. Furthermore, if retirement threatens you with financial hardship, work as long as you can.

Look at Joshua 13:1: "Now Joshua was old and stricken in years; and the Lord said unto him, Thou art old and stricken in years, and there remaineth yet very much land to be possessed."

As long as you live in this world, God has something for you to do.

A guideline on when to retire is to do what will help you to serve the Lord best. You will be happy whether you work or retire if you will enjoy the Lord's presence and leadership and if you will reach up for His energy and power.

Remember that retirement is terminal and it can end quickly. Keeping busy can help you stay alive. Retirement is not a time to quit living. God's statement to Joshua that there is much land to be possessed can apply to you. With whatever strength and years you have left, God has much for you to do. Will you be able to do God's will by retiring or by continuing to work?

Pray for God to help you to know when to retire.

What are the blessings of a long life?

A sixty-year-old woman wrote: "The Bible teaches that a long life is blessed, but I can't see many blessings in getting old."

This woman is realistic. An active person near retirement age can dread getting old. Such an attitude can develop from unpleasant experiences with old people.

As a person over seventy, I can tell you that the situation of the elderly has changed greatly in my lifetime and that the rate of change is accelerating.

I know who asked this question. Life will always be full of blessings for her. In that sense, she will never get old. She is oriented to people and is directed by the Lord. That is the secret of happiness for a youth, an adult in the "best years," and a senior adult.

In senior-adult years most people continue the pattern of life already established. However, the needs people felt in their youth and their prime become more acute. To meet those needs can be more difficult. Your basic characteristics may become more prominent as you age. In senior-adult years a short-tempered person may become even shorter-tempered or a kind person may become even more loving and gentle. People can maintain control of themselves as they age, especially if they practiced self-control through the years.

Proverbs 23:7 says that as people think in their heart so are they.

Pray that in your senior adult years the Lord will bless you by making you a blessing to others.

How can I have the blessings senior adults ought to have?

What you get depends on what you do. Paul gave this advice: "Whatsoever a man soweth, that shall he also reap" (Gal. 6:7). Happiness is like a garden where you reap what you plant. Blessings and happiness come most often from how you feel and what you do. These beatitudes can help.

Beatitudes for Senior Adults

Blessed are senior adults who read their Bible, for they shall find answers to their questions.

Blessed are senior adults who grow in their love for God, for they shall love people more.

Blessed are senior adults who pray for people, for they shall see God do great things.

Blessed are senior adults who wake up looking to Christ the Morning Star, for they will have strength for the day.

Blessed are senior adults who walk in the Light of the World, for they shall not stumble in spirit.

Blessed are senior adults who feast daily on the Bread of Life, for they shall be full of wisdom and joy.

Blessed are senior adults who drink deeply of the Water of Life, for they shall not despair.

Blessed are senior adults who do the work of the Lord, for they shall be paid well.

Blessed are senior adults who love people, for they shall not be lonely.

Pray that you will be a blessing to others and a glory to God.

29

Amazing Grace

How can you prepare for retirement?

Some firms with employees help those approaching retirement. Aging employees learn about things such as Social Security and other benefits, health needs, financial matters, family relationships, retirement centers, and so forth.

People nearing retirement need to prepare wisely for it. Will they need additional income? If so, what can they do to earn some? A man retired who had bought many plants and supplies in a garden store. He asked about working there and was told they could not use him. He came in the next Saturday and the place was crowded. He helped several people get what they wanted and pointed them to a clerk at the register. This happened several weeks and the boss hired him as a Saturday, part-time worker.

Retirement is a time to do what you enjoy.

What about reading? Borrow books or buy used ones.

Do you like television? Watch what you like, but don't let TV take you over and turn you into a "couch potato."

In retirement you may have more control than ever over your time. Time can be worth more than money if used well. Plan to use your time well. Enjoy yourself; help others; and, most of all, do what will glorify God.

What people do in their younger days affects their retirement. That is the meaning of these words from a wise man: "Remember now thy Creator in the days of thy youth, while the evil days come not" (Eccl. 12:1).

Ask God to help you before and during retirement.

Why are some senior adults difficult and others sweet?

Senior adults are like other people. Some are pleasant and gentle and can get along with anybody. Others are difficult and nobody can get along with them.

Every human being has an individual way of looking at things and of reacting to them. That basically is your personality. Some think that one's personality is set fairly early in life and that it develops consistently along those lines unless experiences jolt a person strongly.

A chaplain in a senior-adult center said that the personality of a senior adult changes little unless a drastic chemical imbalance occurs. A major change in circumstances, such as surroundings and relationships, can also disturb someone's personality. In other words, senior adults are apt to behave much as they have all of their lives unless a disturbing change jars them off course.

People who maintain control of their thoughts and emotions can generally maintain a personality consistency better than others.

We can help people in their feelings and behavior toward others. All of us are affected by the way persons around us act. The Bible says, "Iron sharpeneth iron; so a man sharpeneth the countenance of his friend" (Prov. 27:17).

Jesus is our model in personality. He said, "A new commandment I give unto you, That ye love one another; as I have loved you, that ye also love one another" (John 13:34).

Ask God to help you love others as Jesus loves you.

What are the characteristics of senior adults?

An Old Testament wise man warned people to make the most of life because the end could be unpleasant: "However many years a man may live, let him enjoy them all. But let him remember the day of darkness, for they will be many" (Eccl. 11:8, NIV).

What are the senior-adult years like? Whatever you do in those years will involve the family which may include grown children, grandchildren, and great-grandchildren. The family is affected by all that happens to you from the loss of a spouse or other loved ones to one's adjustment to a retirement home.

A major difference for many in the senior-adult period is the loss of occupation along with adjustment to retirement income, which can mean a lower economic living standard. It also means finding things to do to maintain one's interest in life.

Senior adults may experience a decline in physical strength and health which affects everything including one's sex life.

Maintaining social activities in your life calls for planning and effort. You may find help in age groups that schedule leisure activities, develop new interests, recognize the changed social status, and keep concern for civic matters.

Senior adults need to grow in their faith, apply Christian principles to all of life, participate in Bible study and in worship services, witness to others about Christ, have a daily devotion time, and work in the church according to their ability and opportunities.

Ask God to help you in your senior-adult years.

What accounts for the increasing number of senior adults?

Population growth is not a steady numerical increase. Birth rate and extending the average life expectancy both affect the population gain. Things that affect these two factors are medical science, the economic condition, and the social and political situation especially in a time of war. People now entering retirement were born during and immediately after World War I. Those born during the depression years will retire from 1993 to 2005. Then will come a jump in the rate of increase of those entering senior-adult years which will be those born during World War II.

This aging of our society has affected it and will affect it even more in the years ahead. Senior adults will receive more attention. They are now a major factor in the nation's politics and economy. Their growing number creates two problems: How can society meet their needs and also utilize their potential? As the focus turns more on senior adults, they themselves must become more active in solving the problems their presence in society creates.

Two Bible verses within the same chapter seem to contradict each other, but together they say something about these problems: One says, "Bear ye one another's burdens," and the other says "Every man shall bear his own burden" (Gal. 6:2,5). The first admonishes us to care for people who have greater needs than they can take care of. The other verse tells us to take care of our own needs and not be a burden to others.

Ask God to help you be a good member of the growing number of senior adult citizens.

Do people get wiser with age?

Wisdom comes with age. At least, that is what I have always heard. The basis for that hope is an old Roman proverb: "Experience teaches." Job said, "With the ancient is wisdom; and in length of days understanding" (Job 12:12).

The problem with getting wiser is that many people have no idea what wisdom is. Wisdom is not the same as knowledge, but a wise person will seek knowledge. Wisdom in a practical sense is having good judgment. Wisdom looks for the cause behind things, anticipates what things will lead to, evaluates the good or bad in things, and discovers how to effect those causes and results.

To a great extent wisdom does come from experience. Much wisdom happens because people have learning experiences and they learn the lesson. Wisdom can be more deliberate and calculated than that. Be alert to causes and results and also to value and effective actions and you will grow in wisdom and help others.

The Bible is useful in gaining wisdom. "The testimony of the Lord is sure, making wise the simple" (Ps. 19:7). True wisdom responds to the lovingkindness of God. "Whoso is wise, and will observe these things, even they shall understand the lovingkindness of the Lord" (Ps. 107:43).

People in general do not recognize wisdom when they see it. Many of them think it is foolish to follow Christ, but in Christ is where we find real wisdom (1 Cor. 4:10).

Ask God to help you to understand causes and effects and also to know what is good and what you can do about things.

34

The Bible Answers Senior Adults Questions

How can I make my senior-adult years my best years?

The best years are those that are happy. Happiness depends on the spirit within us. If our spirit is controlled by the Holy Spirit, we can meet any situation with strength and hope. The set of your spirit will help you make these years your best.

Guidelines for Happiness

If you as senior adults have learned that happiness comes from loving and being loved, you will have friends and will enjoy life.

Remember that you are children of God and you will be thankful for your blessings and look forward to going home when God is ready for you.

Treasure God's Word, read it daily, and it will comfort you, strengthen you, guide you, and help you enjoy life.

Use what you have to your own good, to help others, and to glorify God and, if you do so, your money or lack of it will not bother you.

Do good things every day and plan ahead for the good things you will do tomorrow and your life will continue to be interesting and exciting.

Keep alert to the presence and power of God in the Holy Spirit and you will overcome fear and loneliness and be a blessing to people around you.

"Let all those that put their trust in thee rejoice: . . . let them also that love thy name be joyful in thee" (Ps. 5:11).

Ask the Lord to bless and guide you so you may be a blessing to others for Him.

Why have I lived so long?

What a good question! Let me share my philosophy of life as a senior adult. I like to call it my credo since it is what I believe.

A Senior Adult's Credo

I believe in a powerful, loving God who has helped me to live this long for a purpose.

I believe God's purpose for senior adults is for them to put back into the lives of younger persons much of the good they themselves received along the way.

I believe in my fellow senior adults who in general have contributed greatly to human progress and to the expansion of freedom in the world.

I believe young people have such potential that they will seek to bring enlightenment and goodness into the world as much or more than we older persons have done.

I believe that God will continue to work through us, as long as we live, to help us to bring people of the world to know Him, to love Him, and to serve Him.

I believe that joy and fulfillment abound for those who do God's will, who care for others, and who walk with the Lord.

The Scripture verse for this credo is Micah 6:8—"He hath showed thee, O man, what is good; and what doth the Lord require of thee, but to do justly, and to love mercy, and to walk humbly with thy God?"

Ask God to help you be sure of what you believe.

3.
Abide with Me

Senior adults have trouble. Some of them have so many problems that they can identify with Job's friend who said, "Man is born to trouble as surely as sparks fly upward" (Job 5:7, NIV). However, for some of them, the trouble they have had is nothing compared to the trouble ahead of them.

People need to be realistic about life. No one knows what tomorrow will bring. My dad told me, "Expect the best but be prepared for the worst." That may not sound like good advice for a youth but it inclined me to optimism that was tempered by realism.

Many problems of senior adults develop from the great changes that aging brings to their lives. The life changes which come with aging occur in almost every area of one's being.

Some of the most obvious problems are those of physical deterioration that come with aging. Ecclesiastes 12 refers to a number of these;

trembling hands (the keepers . . . tremble),

bowed legs (the strong men shall bow),

loss of teeth (the grinders cease because they are few),

diminished vision (those that look out of the windows be darkened), bad hearing (doors shall be shut),

muted voice (daughters of music shall be brought low),

anxiety (afraid of that which is high, and fears shall be in the way),

white hair (the almond tree shall flourish),

failing strength (the grasshopper shall be a burden),

loss of desire (desire shall fail),

approaching death (silver cord be loosed . . . golden bowl be broken . . . dust return to the earth . . . the spirit shall return unto God).

How poetic those words are! They chill me more than they cheer me but they are realistic. In picturesque language they describe the weakened physical condition of a person growing weak in his advanced years. For many senior adults aging is a time of trouble and problems.

Changes threaten us. Will they destroy us? Will they bring pain? Will they deprive us of things we have enjoyed or felt comfortable with? Think of the changes you face and the problems they bring.

A number of the questions that senior adults ask refer to their various problems. Their problems range from those that are real to those that are just imaginary. Some of the real problems have no solution and a person simply has to cope with them the best he can. Then many of the imaginary problems are not easy to handle. They can be harder to cope with than physical pain.

What can you do about problems? An elderly preacher who was a perpetual optimist would grin and say, "Problems are for solving." Set out to solve your problems. Identify them. Analyze them. Plan what you are going to do about problems and tackle them.

A problem can be a blessing by becoming an occasion for you to pray to God, "Abide with me."

Can senior adults do anything to help their memories?

In my twenties I laughed when a man said, "There are three things I can't remember. First is names, second is faces, and—uh—I forget what the third is." People laugh as I tell that joke on myself. However, my memory hasn't got worse; it's always been bad.

A doctor told me memory can be related to one's health. Take good care of yourself. Eat what is good for you; exercise; keep in a good mood; get proper rest. Also stay interested in what happens in the world; associate with people often and stay informed about what they do and how they feel.

Try the following suggestions:

1. Work at remembering. Use your ability to remember or you may lose it.

2. Be sure you understand what you hear and what you read.

3. Relate what you want to remember to things you already know.

4. Repeat what you want to remember immediately either in your mind or aloud.

5. Make notes on a calendar or cards which you can carry or stick on the refrigerator or mirror. Perhaps Peter knew people could forget what he told them and so he wrote two letters. In the second he wrote, "This second epistle, beloved, I now write unto you; in both which I stir up your pure minds by way of remembrance" (2 Pet. 3:1).

Ask God to help you remember the most important things.

What good is retirement for persons whose work was their life?

I preached at the funeral of a man who died at sixty-seven. The funeral home called me because his widow asked for a Baptist preacher. She lived in an apartment that had a window facing a corner shopping center across the street. We talked about her husband. Then she pointed at an easy chair turned toward the window and said, "My husband retired two years ago. He came home, sat down in that chair, and died. It took him two years." She explained further, "All he did was to walk across the street every afternoon, buy more smoking material, and come right back to his chair."

Work is good but there is more to life than work.

Senior adults who have let their work be the major thing in their lives can make something of retirement if they will work at it. Misspent retirement can be as bad or worse than misspent youth.

One of retirement's values is time. I am amazed at how many retirees say that they are busier in retirement than ever. I respond by saying, "Good!"

Senior adults keep busy taking care of themselves; seeing to needs about the house, church, and community; giving time to hobbies; going places locally and away from home; and helping people such as family, neighbors, and needy persons.

The essence of living is deciding things and doing things.

One of my favorite Scripture verses says, "For me to

live is Christ, and to die is gain" (Phil. 1:21).

Ask the Lord to guide you in the use of your time.

How do you adjust to life in a retirement home?

Retirement housing is much better than the county poor farms of fifty years ago. Like anything else, these facilities range from inadequate to four-star ratings.

Find out what is available in your area or where you would like to live. Visit some of the places. Your family might be able to work with you in surveying the possibilities.

Senior-adult housing ranges from complete independence for you to complete care. Some facilities have graduated provisions where you first move into an apartment and take full care of yourself, coming and going as you please. When needs change, you move to another area where you get limited care and then, as needed, you move to another room where you can get complete care.

Recognize your own need and the love of the family in their concern for your comfort and care. Work with them to the extent that it is helpful and express your appreciation for their love and care.

These suggestions will help you adjust:

1. Get acquainted with your space and furnishings.
2. Learn the regulations and the schedule of things.
3. Make friends with the attendants and other residents.
4. Keep in contact with family and friends.
5. Remember Jesus promised to be with you everywhere.
6. Think about Paul's statement: "I have learned, in whatsoever state I am, therewith to be content" (Phil. 4:11).

Ask God to bless the people around you.

What can senior adults do about their reduced income?

Who is kidding whom? Experts talk about the "fixed income" of retired persons. That may be an accurate term but it fools a lot of people. "Fixed income" refers to an annual income that does not change. That sounds like you have a standard of living that doesn't change. This is simply not true. If your income is "fixed" or unchanging, your level of living falls the same amount as the cost of living rises.

This problem has two possible solutions. One is to supplement your income and the other is to limit your buying.

A good place to begin is to keep track of your expenses. Note what purchases or bills are essentials and nonessentials. Keep such a record that you know at some point each month whether you are better or worse off that month. Control your expenditures so you can save and do something extra once in awhile.

Some senior adults may be able to increase their income by doing things to supplement it such as babysit, make salable items, and do odd jobs.

Resolve to enjoy the simple things of life, such as yard work, crafts, walking, church work, visiting people, and especially visiting the sick.

Learn from Paul's attitude about changing circumstances. He said, "I know both how to be abased, and I know how to abound: every where and in all things I am instructed both to be full and to be hungry, both to abound and to suffer need" (Phil. 4:12).

Ask God to help you enjoy your life situation as it is.

Is it wrong to get angry?

Everyone gets mad sometimes or should. Anger rises when something offends you so much that you want to eliminate it or destroy it. Anger can be good because some things should upset us so much that we would do all we could to get rid of them.

What I have said so far sounds like a justification for anger. Some anger is justifiable but we should control our temper and all of our anger. Paul advised, "Be ye angry and sin not: let not the sun go down upon your wrath" (Eph. 4:26). Some insist this is not a command but a concession. Paul's statement means this: if you are angry, don't let it make you sin.

People defend anger by pointing out that God's anger was so intense it was called wrath. However, human anger seldom uses God for a model. James wrote, "Let every man be swift to hear, slow to speak, slow to wrath: for the wrath of man worketh not the righteousness of God" (Jas. 1:19-20).

Anger gives your body a surge of energy to help meet a problem that might be dangerous. If that energy is not needed or if it is used wrongly, it can be harmful to your physical system and even affect your ability to think logically. Furthermore, anger arouses within you feelings of hostility and hatred.

You *can* control your anger. God will help you.

The Bible says, "Cease from anger, and forsake wrath: fret not thyself in any wise to do evil (Ps. 37:8).

Ask God's forgiveness of your wrongful anger and His help in being patient with people.

How can senior adults control their anger?

I can talk to you about this from personal experience. In my youth I realized that I had a short temper. Like some others with short tempers, my flare-up would be hot. Some people have short tempers that explode with heat and then are soon over. My temper wasn't like that. Not only was my temper easily triggered but it would burn hotly for a long time. When it would finally simmer down, I could simply think about the matter and the anger would flame up hot again.

Controlling anger begins with realizing it can be controlled and setting yourself to control it. The Bible says, "Be not hasty in thy spirit to be angry: for anger resteth in the bosom of fools" (Eccl. 7:9).

Recognize that unreasonable anger is hazardous. Jesus said, "Whosoever is angry with his brother without a cause shall be in danger of the judgment" (Matt. 5:22).

Trust to God those things that anger you. "Avenge not yourselves, but rather give place unto wrath: for it is written, Vengeance is mine; I will repay, saith the Lord" (Rom. 12:19).

I still have a distance to go in controlling my temper, but whatever progress I have made has come from asking God to help me love people. Paul said "I pray, that your love may abound yet more and more"(Phil. 1:9).

Ask God to help you grow in love for people. God will do that if you want Him to and that love will help you to control your temper. At least, that has been my experience.

What can I do about declining health and strength?

One senior adult said, "My head makes dates that my feet can't keep." Another one said, "I don't mind going out at night if I can be sure I'll be home by 9 o'clock bedtime." A well-known saying states that, as you grow older, you get weaker and wiser. I am not sure about getting wiser but I am about getting weaker.

People who take care of themselves physically will usually be glad in their senior-adult years that they did so. Neglect your health and your senior years will likely be painful and gloomy. Here are things that are important to your health and well-being:

1. Good nutrition. Eat right. What you eat affects every part of your body and everything you do.

2. Good exercise. Learn what you must do to stimulate your heart, circulation, breathing, and digestion. Then do it.

3. Good rest. Rest enough and sleep well but do not neglect physical activity, mental stimulation, and social relationships.

4. Good mental stimulation. Pay attention to people when they talk; watch good television programs; and read interesting material. Keep your mind open and use it.

5. Good spirits. Maintain a pleasant attitude and disposition. Love God dearly and love people truly. Don't get peeved and grumpy.

Staying well and in good spirits may be more than you think you can do. Paul's words can help you: "I can do all things through Christ which strengtheneth me" (Phil. 4:13).

Ask God to help you want to take good care of yourself and to guide you in getting any help you need.

What can I do about not sleeping well?

Senior adults differ in their sleep needs. Some require little while others need a long night's sleep plus an afternoon nap.

A seventy-year-old woman who has trouble going to sleep at night tried several things and finally found one that helped. After she tells her husband good night, she closes her eyes and begins to sing silently in her mind. No, she is not a singer and even hesitates to participate in congregational singing at church but she loves music. Her silent singing works, not quite 100 percent but nearly. She sings mostly devotional hymns. This helps her go to sleep and blesses her soul and helps her attitude.

Here are some other suggestions:

1. Keep a regular sleep schedule as much as possible.

2. Be active during the day, particularly in the late afternoon.

3. Try snacking before bedtime, particularly on carbohydrates such as cookies. Avoid coffee late in the day.

4. Develop some prebedtime habits, such as watching the late news, reading your Bible, checking the doors and windows, and praying.

5. Occupy your mind and spirit with pleasant thoughts and happy feelings.

If these simple things do not help, see your doctor.

Listen to the Lord's advice to Israel: "Ask where the good way is, and walk in it, and you will find rest for your souls" (Jer. 6:16, NIV).

Ask God to help you sleep in order to serve Him tomorrow.

What is the greatest problem among senior adults?

Someone asked me, "What is the greatest problem among senior adults?" Without knowing of any scientific surveys I answered, "I think the greatest problem for senior adults or for anybody would be the loss of self-esteem. A problem similar to that would be the feeling of uselessness."

I shared this thought with a professional counselor and he said that any kind of loss is a problem to senior adults. He mentioned three other problems which he thought should be listed along with loss: fear, insecurity, and guilt.

A woman who directs activities for senior adults said she was most aware of their fear. They fear both physical and mental decline. They are afraid to make new friends for fear they might make obligations they could not keep. Some are afraid to speak up or participate in things for fear of embarrassment. Some withdraw completely because they are afraid they might have a physical malfunction that would embarrass them and be a problem to others. Much of their fear is insecurity related to self-esteem.

The problem of each senior adult is unique, but problems in general can be approached from a single point. Senior adults and those who work with them can start from that single point in seeking to solve problems. That starting point is love. The Bible says, "There is no fear in love. But perfect love drives out fear, because fear has to do with punishment. The man who fears is not made perfect in love" (1 John 4:18, NIV).

Ask God to help you to approach problems with love.

What can I look forward to as I grow older?

(Note: After I wrote the following answer, I asked my wife this question without showing her my answer. Her response was so stimulating that I am sharing it with you after mine.)

1. We tell small children how wonderful it will be to get older and start to school. Then we point them to the next stage when as youth they will get to drive the car. We promise that college will be even better and that getting a job and getting married will usher them into full adulthood. We help them look forward to such achievements as having children, buying a home, making good at their work, winning recognition from others, and receiving appreciation from family and friends. We keep pointing to the next step. We speak brightly of retirement and complete freedom.

OK. I have made it to seventy and past. What do I have to look forward to? I laugh and say, "I have realized that retirement is terminal." People smile in tolerance and look like they wish I would not say such things.

Let me tell you what we senior adults have to look forward to in every passing decade. As Jesus saw His death rapidly approaching, He said, "I must work the works of him that sent me, while it is day: the night cometh, when no man can work"(John 9:4). Let us look forward to what God has for us to do tomorrow and next week.

When Jesus arose from the dead, He appeared to two of His disciples "as they walked" (Mark 16:12). Young or old, we can look forward to walking every day with our living Lord.

Ask the Lord to help you be aware of His presence and love.

(Note: My wife is more practical than I am and her answer shows that.)

2. When I shared this question with my wife, she asked, "Do you want me to tell you what senior adults can look forward to?"

She and I do not think in the same way. I am logical and she is intuitive. As a logical person, I did not greatly respect intuition, but I have learned—from my wife. Logical persons need to listen to intuitive people. They may learn things they would never have discovered through reasoning.

When my wife offered to give her opinion, I nodded to encourage her.

She said, "Senior adults can look forward to having grandchildren and then to watching them grow, mature, and do good things."

I liked what she said. I raised my eyebrows, gave her an upside-down smile, and laughed with a snort.

She cocked her head and continued, "If senior adults do not have grandchildren, let them watch children and youth grow who are in their church or neighborhood. That will give them something to look forward to."

God's command supports the interest one generation should have in the next: "God blessed them and said to them, 'Be fruitful and increase in number; fill the earth and subdue it' " (Gen. 1:28, NIV).

Ask God to bless the children in your church and neighborhood.

What can I do about being lonely?

Loneliness is fairly common with older people. However they are not the only persons who experience it. Neglected and abused children can suffer deep loneliness. Some teenagers and young people experience loneliness that destroys their self-esteem and drives them to suicide. Look at other adults, at a battered wife or an overburdened husband, whose loneliness is sinking into depression that will need professional attention.

Several things cause senior adults to be lonely. Loss of work, of income, and of social standing may rob them of their purpose and self-respect, and that makes them lonely. Unsure of themselves, they are lonely. Feeling that no one cares for them and pitying themselves, they are lonely. Thinking the world would not miss them and wondering if God even remembers them, they are lonely.

Senior adults at the bottom end of this track need the immediate help of family, church, and doctors.

If you are starting along this track, use the times you are alone to do good things. Spend an hour a day reading your Bible and praying. Spend an hour or more a day enjoying yourself by reading, listening to the radio or television. Keep your living quarters in good order. Contact someone daily by visiting, phoning, or writing. Keep in contact with several people regularly and do things to cheer them up.

Read Psalm 23 often. Say it to yourself. "The Lord is my shepherd; I shall not want" (v. 1).

Ask God to help you remember that He is always with you.

I am afraid at night; what can I do?

Fear is a feeling that some danger is about to hurt you. All of us are afraid at some time. As a child I was afraid of the dark, and I still feel uneasy in a dark place that is strange to me.

In general people are afraid in two particular situations: in the dark and when they are alone. These are real but also symbolic. Facing the unknown (the dark) is frightening and so is facing things alone.

What can you do about fear? Don't be ashamed of it. Fear is as natural as happiness and love. Fear can alert you, energize you, and sharpen your senses to help you escape whatever danger threatens you.

Take precautions to protect yourself. Make your living quarters secure. If the place where you live is not secure, then move.

Do not expose yourself to danger in places you go, where you drive and park, or where you walk.

You are responsible to God to take the best care of yourself that you can. Share your fear with persons you can trust and seek their advice.

If you are afraid of things that are unlikely to happen, here is a Scripture verse that can help: "Fear thou not; for I am with thee: be not dismayed; for I am thy God: I will strengthen thee; yea, I will help thee; yea, I will uphold thee with the right hand of my righteousness" (Isa. 41:10).

Ask God to give you courage; then trust Him and be courageous.

How can I keep from worrying so much?

A pioneer preacher said, "Worry insults God and much of it is a downright sin."

Some people worry as a pastime. What else would they have to do? They don't enjoy worrying, but it beats doing nothing.

Worry is troubling your mind about some problem which doesn't even have to be a real threat. It does not necessarily seek a solution although it may turn in that direction. If it does, it ceases to be worry and becomes problem solving.

Worry is generally useless and consists primarily of annoyance at something which you can do little about. It can be hazardous since it can deteriorate into fretting and then into anxiety.

As with most things, you can control worry. Don't do it. If you worry, set up some guidelines. (This is meant to be funny).

Guidelines for Worrying

1. Worry only when you are in a good mood.
2. Worry in the daytime and never at night.
3. Worry at one time about all the things you have to worry about.
4. Worry on schedule for less than a half hour and quit on time.
5. Do something else when the time for worrying is up.
6. If you worry, enjoy it. Sing or whistle while you do it!
7. Tell everyone how much you worry and what a waste it is.

"Do not worry about tomorrow, for tomorrow will worry about itself. Each day has enough trouble of its own" (Matt. 6:34, NIV).

Ask God to help you use your energy to do good rather than waste it worrying.

How can you tell if you have a senior adult disease?

A man in his twenties often razzed his fifty-year-old father-in-law about getting "see-nile."

Senility is another term for second childhood. So is dotage. However, today's professionals generally do not use these terms which used to refer to the changing personality of older people when they became forgetful and acted childishly. They say there really isn't such a thing as second childhood. What happens is that adults suffer diseases or disruptions that change the way they feel about things and the way they react to them.

Alzheimer's disease is the most widely known of the illnesses which show up primarily in memory loss and disorientation. A number of diseases have such symptoms and can begin earlier in life than in senior adulthood. Many of them are similar to Alzheimer's but are treatable. Because of mistaken ideas senior adults fail to seek diagnosis and treatment about memory and disorientation problems that are reversible.

Every person needs a doctor who can give periodical examinations and advise how to keep the body at the peak of efficiency. Failing to take care of your God-given body is worse than failing to take care of a costly automobile.

Senior adults have lived long enough to know to take care of themselves. Look at Psalm 90 which is called a prayer of Moses. "So teach us to number our days, that we may apply our hearts unto wisdom" (v. 12).

Ask God to give you wisdom in caring for yourself.

4.
This Is My Father's World

We senior adults are part of our world. We have seen more changes in that world than any other generation has seen. As children, we watched blacksmiths put iron shoes on horses. We learned about World War I from men who fought in it. We would run out of the house to watch an airplane fly over. We rode in the Model T and thought a great, new day had come when the Model A could go sixty miles per hour. We remember Lindbergh's flight, the Great Depression, FDR, and the beginning of Social Security. Many who are now senior adults served in World War II.

We listened to radio, cheered when movies became "talkies," and now glue ourselves to television.

The world has changed and we had a part of it. None of the nations we studied in our big geography books have escaped great changes.

No other senior adults in all history had the advantages and life services we have today. People used to die in their forties and fifties from what are now minor ailments. Flu epidemics once devastated older people. Now we get "flu shots" and would not know about the epidemics if it were not for the news media.

This is a great day for senior adults. But some would

say things are not that good for each elderly person.

We senior adults have problems those before us never dreamed of. Long life sounds like a blessing but it brings unanticipated difficulties. For over a century now society has scrambled to adjust to the changes that have come with scientific progress, with modern social concepts, and with political pressures no group ever exerted before.

Senior adults should have a better perspective on the changes than anyone else. However, that is not necessarily true. People can find change difficult unless they feel that the changes are needed to make their situation acceptable and hopefully better.

Many adults stopped on some comfortable plateau in their mental and spiritual growth. I know a fellow who is a sixty-five-year-old juvenile. Acting like you are thirteen is great if that is your age but acting like thirteen when you are sixty or seventy is not so good. Let us senior adults take pleasure and pride in our age.

We senior adults have increased in number. Our financial needs and desires have become a nightmare to politicians.

We have been told not to ask what our country can do for us but rather to ask what we can do for our country. That is political rhetoric. A country exists primarily for the good of its citizens. We cannot lay aside our expectations of help but we must indeed match those with our commitment to make this nation and our world the kind of place God the Creator wants it to be. On one hand let us ask our country to help us and on the other let us also ask what we can do for our country. In doing that we shall rise above ourselves and we must do that.

Why do senior adults act the way they do?

Some think senior adults are different from other adults and they don't know what to do with them. Many senior adults themselves feel they are different but don't know why.

Senior adults are like other age groups when it comes to the basic motives of life. The difference is in the circumstances and the individual experiences of persons. Senior adults have an accumulation of experiences that affect how they look on things and also how they react to things.

Senior adults want to live as long as they can, and they want security and comfort. They want people to respect them and to care for them. They want to feel that their lives mean something. They also want to have a sense of fulfillment.

Part of all of this, or perhaps the total sum of it, is the matter of self-esteem. The esteem you have for yourself comes largely from how you think others feel about you.

Senior adults do what they feel they have to do in order to live, to be secure and comfortable, to win respect and love, to do something worthwhile, and to keep growing. Along with this they work hard to maintain their self-esteem and dignity.

Like everyone else senior adults do not always achieve the desired results from what they do. They may be like Paul who said, "The good that I would I do not: but the evil which I would not, that I do" (Rom. 7:19). He also said, "I can do all things through Christ which strengtheneth me" (Phil. 4:13).

Pray for God's guidance in all you do.

How can senior adults help each other and people in general?

Two major factors are involved in helping people. First, what do they seem to need? Second, how much do you feel you can do for them?

Everybody has emotional needs. When people do not get their emotional needs met, they have emotional problems. Nearly every person has some emotional problems at times. If people understood their emotional problems and would express themselves, they would probably scream, "Please, will somebody love me?"

Because of the experience of senior adults, they may have great ability to love people. Love means to do what you can for a person's good. Grandparents and other older relatives have rescued and strengthened younger relatives by their love. This love will not be a dominating love but rather a love that looks for the good in you, commends those good qualities, and expresses confidence that you will rise to your potential.

Strengthening others by loving them has its rewards. Most senior adults themselves feel the need for the living support of others. Meet the need of others for love and you will in return receive the loving support you need. It will come from those you love.

Jesus Himself told how much we should love people: "A new commandment I give unto you, That ye love one another; as I have loved you, that ye also love one another" (John 13:34).

Ask God to help you love others, to see the good in them, and to encourage them with loving commendations.

Why doesn't God do something about the world's problems?

God has already done something about sins and troubles in the world. To begin with He created moral creatures who would have a sense of value and beauty. These moral creatures were human beings who classify things as right or wrong and make moral choices in their actions. They shape their own personalities morally.

Without such ability we would not know things are good or bad, right or wrong. The sense of right and wrong lifts human beings to a high place in creation. Things in the natural order, like floods and earthquakes, have no meaning except as they affect human beings. A world with problems is a great challenge to people.

God could have set people in the world and left them to survive or perish but He did not do that. He stayed in the world and gives us guidance and help as we seek to cope with the problems of the world. He does not violate human freedom. He helps us grow to be more like His Son, our Lord Jesus Christ.

Jesus said, "My Father worketh hitherto, and I work" (John 5:17). "Hitherto" means "up to this moment." How does God work? He made a world of order, set up laws, sent His Son to be our Lord, assigned His Holy Spirit to be with us for knowledge and power, leads us and answers our prayers to the extent that helps us fulfill our potential, and sets a time for evaluation and judgment.

Finally, He authorized us to enlist everyone in the fight against evil and promised His constant presence.

Ask God to help you do all you can to bless others and to glorify the Lord.

What can senior adults do about what's happening in the world?

The future belongs to the younger generation. However senior adults are increasing and can have a major voice in shaping that future. Politicians think this is true.

Senior adults must learn from other voting blocs. Some of those insisted so greatly on their own interests that they became a threat to other people. We senior adults are strong enough now to affect how things go.

Here are actions we can take in order to affect things:

1. Keep informed through television, newspapers, and magazines.

2. Share your interests and concerns with others.

3. Write letters to editors of publications.

4. Write to state and national officials.

5. Apply Bible teachings to local, national, and world matters.

6. Encourage others to pray and to express their concern.

A good guideline is the answer the lawyer gave to Jesus when Jesus asked him what the Bible said about how to have eternal life. The lawyer quoted from the Old Testament: "Thou shalt love the Lord thy God with all thy heart, and with all thy soul, and with all thy strength, and with all thy mind; and thy neighbour as thyself" (Luke 10:27).

When the lawyer asked Jesus who a person's neighbor was, Jesus told him about a terrorized Jewish traveler who was helped by a Samaritan merchant. We are to do something about the world's problems and also those near at hand.

Ask God to guide you to persons whom you might help.

What will the rapid increase of senior adults mean?

In two decades persons over sixty-five increased in number twice as fast as the rest of the population. Now, in America one out of nine persons is over sixty-five, and within a few decades that ratio will become one out of five.

Two things contribute to this rapid increase. One is the population explosion in the past hundred years. The other is an extension of the average life expectancy because of medical advances.

Here is what that can mean to the nation and world:

1. Senior adults influence national politics. They are a powerful bloc of voters that politicians cannot ignore. Senior adults now lobby primarily for their own interests. However, they will soon influence every phase of national government.

2. Senior adults affect the country's economy. Pressure for health care and life benefits can shape the national budget. Will senior adults think of the nation's good as well as their own?

3. Senior adults will change the labor situation. Many will keep working and some will go back to work. Furthermore, their desires and buying patterns will affect production and marketing.

4. Conflict may develop between senior adults and younger people in political control, economy, education, and entertainment.

The Bible says the glory of age is in responsible living: "The hoary head is a crown of glory, if it be found in the way of righteousness" (Prov. 16:31).

Ask God to use senior adults in making this a better world.

Should we worry about youth turning from our values?

Throughout human history every generation has worried about the younger generation. Even the ancient Greeks wrote about their youth departing from the standards that previous generations had cherished.

In the 1930s, in my teens, evangelists used to make young people their targets. Some said the youth were "going to the dogs." Others defended young people and insisted they were some of the best persons in all of time.

Youth and senior adults are alike in some ways. Both groups are in a stage of great change and adjustment. Youth are no longer children; nor are they yet fully adult. People expect them to behave as adults and, if they don't, they scold the youth as though they were still children.

Senior adults can help youth and the youth can help senior adults. Let each generation look for the good in the other and enjoy what they find.

Note the advice a man of years gave to a young man:

> Rejoice, O young man, in thy youth; and let thy
> heart cheer thee in the days of thy youth, and
> walk in the ways of thy heart, and in the sight of
> thine eyes: but know thou, that for all these things

God will bring thee into judgment (Eccl. 11:9).

Paul said to young Timothy, "Let no man despise thy youth; but be thou an example of the believers, in word, in conversation, in charity, in spirit, in faith, in purity" (1 Tim. 4:12).

Ask God to help you love and encourage young people.

What do people in general think of senior adults?

These questions reflect some of the mistaken ideas people have about senior adults:

1. Have senior adults passed the age of usefulness? Can people accept their advice, depend on them, or use them? Aging does not deprive persons of their mental and physical abilities. Disease does that and it can damage people of any age.

2. Are senior adults a financial liability to families and to the nation? Are older people worth what they cost society? To begin with, many elderly persons are financially independent and live in their own houses. In the second place they are the ones who helped finance a century of progress and are worthy of some of the resulting benefits.

3. Are senior adults frail and sickly? Like other people some senior adults are not well and others are. Usually, the better care they take of themselves, the better they get along.

4. Do most senior adults wind up in nursing homes? Few senior adults, less than 5 percent, are in such homes and many pay for their keep.

Paul said, "My God will supply every need of yours according to his riches in glory in Christ Jesus" (Phil. 4:10).

An older person in the Bible said, "Cast me not off in the time of old age; forsake me not when my strength faileth" (Ps. 71:9).

Ask God to help senior adults and people in general to understand each other and to be mutually helpful.

At what age should senior adults quit driving cars?

Quit driving if you are a risk to yourself and a danger to others.

Here are guidelines to help you in driving:

1. Watch other cars around you. Be alert and aware of other drivers and of potential problems. Two major problems for some older drivers are judging the speed of oncoming cars and seeing cars on either side of you.

2. Have your eyes checked regularly. Do not let any problem with your vision go uncared for.

3. Be sure you know what effect your medications have. Do not drive if your medications make you drowsy and slow to react to a problem.

4. Drive where you feel safe and at times of the day that are easiest for you. Avoid freeways if changing lanes and if speed bother you. Drive at night only if you can see well. Keep your driver's license up to date.

5. On a trip have at least one other driver along with whom you share driving time.

6. If you buy a car, get one you feel comfortable in, one you can see out of adequately, and one with mirrors and instruments easy to see and reach.

Be realistic about your abilities and disabilities. Paul said, "I have learned the secret of being content in any and every situation" (Phil. 4:12, NIV).

Ask the Lord to keep you sensitive to what's around you.

What if no one wants anything from you?

The time can come for senior adults when they feel that nobody needs anything from them.

A woman who moved had some things she valued but she had no place for them in her new home. She didn't want to discard them and so she put them away on a high shelf. Senior adults can feel like those treasured objects. People still seem to care for them but put them on a shelf and do not use them.

Some senior adults with wisdom and skill feel they are passed over. They feel they still have something to offer but no one wants them. They feel overlooked and neglected.

Senior adults who have ideas and abilities to share do not need to sit around and wish for someone to enlist them. They themselves are at the edge of one of the greatest needs today. That need is ministry to senior adults.

A worker with senior adults says that senior adults are generally reluctant to help each other. This may be because they are afraid they might do something wrong or offend. As one senior adult, set yourself to help others in your age bracket. Take the lead if you are willing. Get what you need and do things for senior adults or for anybody. If you prefer not to lead, then assist a leader in doing things for senior adults. Maybe you will need help and can enlist a friend to help you.

"Whatsoever thy hand findeth to do, do it with thy might" (Eccl. 9:10).

Ask God to help you be useful wherever you are.

Is it wrong for senior adults to drink?

The guards asked a man in prison on the day before his execution what he would like for his last meal. He ordered steak with mushrooms and explained he had always wanted to try mushrooms but had been afraid of them. Laughing, he said, since this was his last meal, if they killed him, he wouldn't miss much.

Some senior adults may feel that, since they are nearing the end of life, they just as well live with abandon and do anything. If they have such an attitude, they ought to consider at least two things.

One is to keep in mind the effect of any action, both immediate and in the long run. We should be good stewards of our physical abilities until the very end of life.

Another thing to consider is the effect of your action on others. A man in his latter years, who suffered a lot of pain and also felt neglected, began drinking heavily as a kind of escape. What did he have to lose at his age? A lot! He lost the respect of some he cared for most, his grandchildren. That is a high price to pay for self-indulgence.

When Caleb in the Old Testament was eighty-five, he asked his friend Joshua to give him the task of conquering a mountain where giants lived. We still quote the request of that old man along with his statement of trust in the Lord: "If the Lord be with me, then I shall be able to drive them out" (Josh. 14:12).

Ask the Lord to help you show those who care for you what a senior adult can do with the Lord's help.

5.

He Leadeth Me

The world is changing and senior adults are also changing. They are learning many new things.

My mother was born in 1882. As far as daily living was concerned, her world was more like that of New Testament times than like our world today. People raised what they ate, wove cloth, and cut trees to make their homes. In travel most walked or depended on animals. In her early teens my mother's family moved from Kentucky to Missouri and she drove one of their three covered wagons, pulled by a team of four oxen. The trip required several weeks.

The energy of steam had been harnessed but it did not affect people's daily routine. In the use of steam to drive boats and trains, people began to get a glimpse of great changes to come.

My mother grew up washing clothes outdoors in a huge iron pot heated over a wood fire. She lived past the middle of the twentieth century to become a television fan and to fly in an airplane.

I saw my mother lose her temper. She heard someone refer to "the good old days" of her youth. She almost exploded, "They can have those good old days! Give me electricity, airplanes, TV, and especially water piped to the kitchen and bathroom."

Undreamed of changes have come and have affected all of us more than we realize. We senior adults might like for changes to slow down but they probably won't. More likely the rapid changes will even speed up.

Continued change will be costly and therefore it will be geared to the national and world economy. That means changes will have to affect the daily lives of people for them to be willing to support the expense of continued advancement.

Senior adults may be more aware of these changes than others because of the perspective they developed in the decades they have lived.

What should senior adults do to fit into their changing world? What attitude should they have for their own sake and also for the good of others? What changes should they themselves make to receive the greatest benefit from what is happening? Is there even any point in older people trying to keep up with what is going on? Why should they? What can they do about things?

Many things are happening that affect our lives now and will make an even greater impact on us in the months ahead. For instance, gadgets flood the market and promise to make our lives safer, easier, more comfortable, and more enjoyable. Discoveries offer us treatment and advice about conquering ills and improving our fitness.

Let's give thought to what these times can mean to us, what we should do to benefit most, what we should to do support good developments, and what we Christians can do in order to bless others and glorify God. That would mean for us to learn new things and to be willing to make some changes.

How can I pray more effectively?

Some churches know their senior adults pray a lot and therefore have enlisted them to be "prayer warriors." Senior adults who are easily accessible by phone can form strong prayer chains.

Prayer is communicating with God.

Can senior adults pray more effectively? Yes, we can. However, let's be careful that an emphasis on effective praying does not discourage people from praying. Encourage people to learn to pray more effectively. Urge them, though, just to pray more.

In whatever way you pray, be aware of the loving presence and great power of God. The Lord's Prayer (Matt. 6:9-13) teaches us to address God: "Our Father which art in heaven." We pray with several objectives in mind.

1. One objective of praying is to praise the Lord and that is a good way to begin prayer. Look at the Lord's Prayer: "Hallowed be thy name."

2. Another objective is submission to God: "Thy kingdom come. Thy will be done in earth, as it is in heaven."

3. Another objective is to ask help for your physical needs, "Give us this day our daily bread"; for your spiritual need of forgiveness, "Forgive us our debts, as we forgive our debtors"; and for personal guidance, "Lead us not into temptation, but deliver us from evil."

Recognize also that God is King and has power and glory.

Ask the Lord to help you to pray in the manner Jesus taught His disciples to pray.

What can I do about how things change and affect my life?

The rate of change in the world has accelerated since United States became a nation over two centuries ago. People then lived much like people before them for 2,000 years. Living conditions, travel, and communication had changed little since Jesus' day. The world's advance in 2,000 years was primarily in ideas about nature and in human relations. These advances came mostly from Greek philosophy and Jesus' teaching.

Scientific and mechanical changes picked up speed in the 1800s and began to affect the practical lives of people. The most dramatic change was learning to use steam to turn wheels and thereby to propel boats and trains. Another significant change was the improvement of printing and distribution of printed material. This speeded up the spread of news and ideas. Scholars communicated more freely and persons with innovative dispositions invented devices that would help society as well as individuals.

Science added quality to daily living. Many changes helped senior adults.

Government theory also changed. Now the whole world wants government "by the people, of the people, and for the people."

Here is what senior adults should do in these changing times. Keep up with the changes but keep in your mind what you believe about God and His purpose in the world. Paul said, "I know whom I have believed, and am persuaded that he is able to keep that which I have committed unto him against that day" (2 Tim. 1:12).

Ask God to help you do His will in these changing times.

How important is one's attitude in these changing times?

Attitude refers to your thoughts and feelings. It is the set of your mind and emotions. Your ongoing attitude is your disposition or way of thinking and acting. Controlling your attitude will help you in these changing times. Make your attitude or disposition be what you want it to be. Here are some guidelines:

1. Laugh when things threaten you or go wrong. You can cry and throw your hands up helplessly or you can grin and bear it. Identify the changes, adjust to them, or work to change them.

2. Face change and study it. Often you will see a way to do something and you will be able to meet it.

3. Tackle changes with determination. When you vigorously throw yourself into something, you will have more power than you thought you could have.

4. Stay at a task long enough to get it done or at least until you have to quit for something else.

5. Trust that changes can be handled. Trust others to prove helpful. Trust yourself and you will find abilities you did not realize you had.

6. Depend on God to help you think, to channel your strength, to reinforce your good relations with others, and to give you the joy of doing a hard job well.

The Bible emphasizes the importance of your disposition and attitudes: "As he [a person] thinketh in his heart, so is he" (Prov. 23:7).

Ask God to help you have a good attitude about change.

What can senior adults do to stay in a cheerful mood?

You can't be cheerful when you are sad. On the other hand, if you are down in the dumps and blue, you need to cheer up.

Some people can shake off depression and force themselves to rejoice and be glad. If you are one of those, good for you!

Can the rest of us be cheerful and stay that way? Let's try these four simple rules:

1. Find something to enjoy every day. It could be something beautiful in nature like the sunshine, rain, flowers, or whatever. It could be something good that you see, hear, touch, taste, or smell. It could be anything that gives you a lift.

2. Discover a treasure of words, some good statement, to hold in your mind for the day. You could memorize a verse of Scripture or a phrase of three or four words that pleases you. You might remember this only a day but you might hold it in your heart the rest of your life.

3. Do some good thing every day for others. Make something for them, write to them, call them, or do whatever you can that they need or would enjoy.

4. Pray for at least two people every day—for someone you dearly love and for someone you dislike or care little for.

These deeds will cheer you up and help you physically and spiritually.

Jesus said to a man, "Son, be of good cheer; thy sins be forgiven thee" (Matt. 9:2).

Ask God to help you cheer up by being a blessing to others.

Can senior adults learn new things?

Now that I am a senior adult, I don't like the saying, "You can't teach an old dog new tricks." I feel like I am the old dog and that they are talking about me.

People's learning ability declines a little but usually that is because they do not keep trying to learn. If you have slipped some in learning, you can regain most of your ability simply by applying yourself.

Take a look at what you have learned in the last several months. Have you learned more about your own needs, your church's plans, your community, the changes in the world? Do you try to find out more about things that come up?

Be specific about what hinders you from learning things nowadays. What is the problem? Do you not care? Are there not things you would like to know more about? What resources would you need to learn what you want to know?

Pick out things you would like to learn to do or things you would like to learn more about. What about developing skill in some sports, a gardening technique, the use of a shop tool, your hobby, how to get the most for your money, ? Then, what about using your community library, making trips to places of interest, or attending senior adult discussion groups, ?

Decide what you need to do to learn what you want to learn. The Bible says, "Commit thy works unto the Lord, and thy thoughts shall be established" (Prov. 16:3).

Ask God to help you learn more about His world and His will.

Do senior adults need to attend church regularly?

Going to church is a good habit. If that is true, look at this list:

Good Things About Attending Church

1. It keeps you aware of the presence, power, and love of God.

2. It encourages you to worship the Lord, to thank Him for His goodness, to praise His glory, and to seek His guidance.

3. It helps you to feel the very presence of Jesus who promised to be with us when we gather in His name.

4. It reminds you to love your fellow church members, even as Christ loved you.

5. It provides you with a way to give and share the gospel with the whole world.

6. It stimulates you to grow in Christlikeness in your own character, in what you do for others, and in your service to God.

7. It helps you to have a positive attitude about life and to meet things with courage.

8. It calls you to open yourself to God through prayer.

9. It says to everyone that you are serious about your faith.

10. It satisfies a deep longing within your soul.

Christ wants you to attend church. The Bible says: "Not forsaking the assembling of yourselves together" (Heb. 10:25); and, "Where two or three are gathered together in my name, there am I in the midst of them" (Matt. 18:20).

Ask God to help you join others regularly in worship.

How mature can senior adults become?

When we were children and youth, adults scolded us saying, "When are you going to grow up? Why don't you act your age?" No one has said that to me for years. Does that mean that at last I am mature? Not necessarily. It may mean folks have given up on me.

Let's test our maturity with these questions:

1. Am I mature enough to love all persons and to keep on loving them the way Christ loves me?

2. Am I mature enough to trust the Lord so much I will do anything He wants me to do?

3. Am I mature enough to keep my hope bright regardless of what happens to me?

4. Am I mature enough to cooperate with my fellow Christians in reaching and teaching people the way Christ commanded?

5. Am I mature enough to give at least as much as God commanded people in the Old Testament to give?

6. Am I mature enough to forgive people and not to hold bad feelings toward them?

7. Am I mature enough to work hard becoming more like Christ?

These Scriptures will help us: "Until we all reach unity in the faith and in the knowledge of the Son of God and become mature, attaining to the whole measure of the fullness of Christ" (Eph. 4:13, NIV). "May the God of peace . . . equip you with everything good for doing his will" (Heb. 13:20-21, NIV).

Ask God to keep you growing in Christian maturity.

Can we control our motives?

Motives are what cause you to act in a certain way. Basically a motive is an inner force that moves you to act. It is a thought or a feeling and in that sense your motivation changes with your experience. Therefore, you can control your motives to the extent that you control ideas and emotions.

How you understand what is around you and how you feel toward it will determine what your life is like. That would include your happiness or misery, your goodness or wickedness, your success or failure, and everything else.

Some say that early in life one idea develops that becomes such a forceful motive that it is almost the only motive. That is the idea and the feeling which you develop about yourself.

Theories differ. They can help us if we realize they are efforts to state the truth.

Here is the truth: "Jesus saith unto him, I am the way, the truth, and the life: no man cometh unto the Father but by me" (John 14:6). "As many as received him [Christ], to them gave he power to become the sons of God, even to them that believe on his name" (John 1:12).

When you receive Jesus Christ as the Son of God and as your Savior, you become a child of God. If you accept this truth as a reality, it will radically change the ideas and feelings you have about yourself and motivate you to do good things that will bless people and glorify your Father in heaven.

Ask God to help you want to be His loving, faithful child.

What can senior adults do about being bored?

A seven-year-old responded to my question about how he liked school by saying, "It's boring." I chuckled and started to tell him how good school could be. He raised his eyebrows and said, "That's boring." I almost exploded laughing but I restrained myself and simply shrugged.

Are you like that boy? Bored and feeling superior because of it. What can you do?

1. Keep physically active. Don't just sit and sigh.

2. Keep mentally active. Pursue things that interest you.

3. Keep spiritually active. Read the Bible, pray, enjoy Christian fellowship, and get involved in Christian service.

4. Study something for a month to six months or a year. For instance, Bible characters, your state history, your hobby, are areas of interest to study..

5. Collect something: Stamps, buttons, signatures, and so forth.

6. Keep in touch with people: relatives, friends, and so forth.

7. Don't put things off. If you do, you will get bored.

8. Try something new, such as food, a game, or entertainment.

9. Make a trip.Go around the world, across town, or somewhere in between.

10. Love people. Pray for them, get in touch with them, do something for them.

"They that wait upon the Lord shall renew their strength" (Isa. 40:31). "The inward man is renewed day by day" (2 Cor. 4:16). "Be renewed in the spirit of your mind" (Eph. 4:23).

Ask God to help you make both your own life interesting and also the lives of others.

What can you do if you have a hard time getting things done?

I have told friends that I will do anything my wife can get me to do.

They always look quickly at her to see if that is true.

She nods and says, "And I can get him to do anything if he wants to do it."

That has become a comedy routine for us and we do it often. Personally, I think it is funny even if we don't get many laughs.

All of us senior adults do about what we want to do. Therefore beds go unmade, dishes stack up in the sink, yards go unmowed and get ragged, and we even fail to take care of our health.

Daily schedules help some people. I read in the magazine *Mature Living* about a couple who give an hour a day to their souls and in that time they pray, meditate, and read the Bible. They give an hour a day to their bodies when they walk, swim, or ride their bikes. They also give an hour a day to their minds when they read. Then they give themselves the rest of the day off. I didn't adopt their schedule but it sounds good and I recommend it.

Have some things that you do regularly every day. Don't put these off. Besides that decide the day before or the first thing in the morning what you will do on a day. If you need motivation, invite somebody over several days ahead of time. That's when we clean house—when company is coming.

"There is a time . . . for every work" (Eccl. 3:17).

Ask God to help you do both your work and also His work.

What should be the priorities of senior adults?

The manager of a business sets priorities to help bring success to the work he manages. God assigns work to us.

Consider this list of priorities:

Commitment to the Lord.

• Do God's will and do it well.

• Ask God to give you wisdom and power to do His will. Use the Bible as your guide.

Commitment to people.

• Love people, win them, train them, lead them.

• As people do things for you and do their work well, show your appreciation.

Commitment to what should be done.

• Understand the objectives and the value of God's work.

• Use resources well and cheerfully give what you have.

Commitment to cooperation.

• Work with others to please the Lord.

• Help Christians to appreciate each other and to co-operate in doing God's work.

Commitment to yourself.

• Keep well informed, energized, faithful, and happy.

The Bible says: "Whatsoever thy hand findeth to do, do it with thy might" (Eccl. 9:10) and "What doth the Lord require of thee, but to do justly, and to love mercy, and to walk humbly with thy God" (Mic. 6:8)?

Ask God to help you put first things first.

6.

Are Ye Able?

Senior adults can do a lot of things.

Jeff D. Ray was a Baptist pastor in early Texas days. When B. H. Carroll started Southwestern Baptist Theological Seminary, he enlisted Ray to teach young preachers to preach. At eighty Ray still taught when I enrolled there in 1940. Most students loved him and called him Uncle Jeff.

Uncle Jeff dressed sharply, spoke distinctly, and used a lot of personal illustrations. One day he chuckled as he began his lecture, "Boys, a student just asked me when does a man get so old that he quits admiring the pretty girls."

Uncle Jeff laughed deep in his throat and said, "I told him I didn't know."

The class roared with laughter and he turned his head from side to side, grinning broadly, and laughed with them.

Senior adults keep most of their desires, abilities, and interests unless disease or negative experiences disrupt them.

Many have mistaken ideas about the senior adult stage of life. Some dread it greatly. They think life ends at retirement. They dread not having anything to do, wonder if they can live on their income, and worry about becoming ill or disabled. What if they lose their independence and spend years in humiliating decline?

At the other extreme a few have an unrealistic idea that they will have absolute freedom and spend all their time doing just what they want to do.

On the day I retired, the office folk had a party for me and my wife at 3 o'clock. She and I left the building at 4, took care of several things, and exactly at 5 PM we stopped for a red light at an intersection.

Glancing at my watch, I shouted loudly, "Free! Free at last!"

My wife smirked, laid her hand on my knee, and said, "No, you're not! You belong to me."

We both laughed the rest of the way home.

As you become a senior adult, two opposite truths are so. Everything is different but nothing has changed.

Figure out that paradox and you will do well as a senior adult.

You and your circumstances will be extensions of what has been before. However you will have new experiences and face new problems and opportunities. Trust yourself and above all, trust the Lord. Along with that, love people. Ask the Lord to help you love Him more. Then ask Him to help you love people the way that He loves you.

The secret to doing well as a senior adult is the same as in any previous stage of life. Do what is right, love other persons dearly, and deepen your relationship with the Lord. In senior adulthood keep doing the good you have done and keep doing what you do well. Stop doing whatever you have been doing that is wrong, and if possible, don't do those things you do poorly.

With their limitations, what can senior adults do for the Lord?

Some people think senior adults can't do much church work. Senior adults contribute to that opinion by their own attitudes. We senior adults differ greatly in what we can do. Some serve on committees, teach, and do anything anyone else can do. Only you can decide what you can do and you will need God's help in that.

Recognize your limitations. You may not have the strength and income you once had. Be thankful for what you can do. Look at these suggestions as possibilities.

1. Live daily as a Christian should.

2. Read your Bible and other good literature.

3. Pray for your family, friends, neighbors, sick persons, church leaders, our country, and so forth. Update your prayer list weekly.

4. Contact people by visiting, by telephoning, or by writing. Give them Christian literature.

5. Telephone people, tell them about Christ, and invite them to church. Send them gospel tracts.

6. Encourage others by expressing appreciation to them.

7. Cheerfully give your tithes and offerings.

8. Keep informed about what your church is doing.

9. Share your faith and love for God with persons you see.

10. Add your own specific items to this list.

Paul said, "Make it your ambition to lead a quiet life, to mind your own business, and to work with your hands, as we commanded you" (1 Thess 4.11, NIV).

Thank God for what you can do and ask His help in doing it.

How can we pray and be sure our prayers will be answered?

Jesus said we could pray and receive what we asked for if we would do two things. Look at those two promises:

1. "All things, whatsoever ye shall ask in prayer, believing, ye shall receive" (Matt. 21:22).

A faith healer failed to help a paralyzed invalid who came to him. The healer told the crowd the problem was the sick man's lack of faith. The invalid went home disappointed, but he loved the Lord greatly and praised Him daily for His care. I have never known a man with greater faith than that witness.

Faith is not wishing; nor is it a kind of magic where you say certain words with enough feeling and get what you want.

Faith is committing yourself to God for Him to do what is best for you and what will be the greatest blessing to others. Faith does not dictate to God; it yields completely to God's will. Anyone who really wants God's will done in his life will get what he wants.

2. "Whatsoever ye shall ask the Father in my name, he will give it you" (John 16:23).

I like to close a prayer by saying, "We ask this in Jesus' name," but I realize that statement may not affect my prayer one bit. These are not magic words which obligate God to give you what you ask for. In fact, it is not the words "in Jesus' name" that make it actually in Jesus' name. It is, rather, that our attitude and our requests be in tune with what Jesus would want for us. Prayer is like a check. Unsigned, a check is no good. Prayer that is not "in Jesus' name" is not effective. We are to pray for what Jesus Himself would sign His name to.

Pray in the name of Jesus and pray with faith.

What happens to love when senior adults no longer have sex?

Some couples continue sexual activity into their advanced years while some stop much earlier. Openly discussing their sexual needs and desires will help most aging couples.

Paul said, "The husband should fulfill his marital duty to his wife, and likewise the wife to her husband. Do not deprive each other except by mutual consent and for a time, so that you may devote yourself to prayer" (1 Cor. 7:3,5, NIV).

In these times people confuse love and sex. They say they made love when what they did was to have sexual intercourse. Sex is a physical action with a pleasing effect. In that sense it is like eating or sleeping. Sex may be an expression of love, but it can be just the opposite.

Love is a misused term in this day. Love is caring for someone so much you are not happy unless that person cares for you. Love seeks satisfaction from the beloved and also seeks to satisfy the beloved. Love has several levels, and at its highest you will do anything possible for the good of your beloved and will let your beloved do anything possible for your good.

Sex is an essential if the lovers need it, but it is not if the lovers don't need it.

Love may have several essentials but three basics are:

1. Finding pleasure in each other's presence
2. Being interested on each other's ideas and actions
3. Enjoying doing things for each other

Ask God to bless your loving relationship with your spouse.

How can senior adults witness to people about Christ?

Senior adults may have less opportunity to witness because of their circumstances. However, some have a greater opportunity because they have more control of their time than they once had.

1. For those who do not have much opportuny to witness: share with those whom you do see. Lovingly and briefly tell them what Christ means to you, quote a Scripture to them, and give them a tract. Your church may have tracts you can use.

2. For people who are as busy as ever: set a time to go witnessing with someone. Busy people do what they plan to do and what they promise they will do.

3. For those busier than ever: make witnessing one of your highest priorities and set some goals. Your goals could be the amount of time you would witness and the number of people you would try to witness to.

Here are helpful guidelines:

1. Memorize soul-winning verses such as John 3:16; John 5:24; and Romans 10:9.

2. Love God and love people.

3. Pray before you witness, while you do so, and afterward.

4. Tell others about your witnessing experiences and encourage them also to witness.

"They that be wise shall shine as the brightness of the firmament; and they that turn many to righteousness as the stars forever and ever" (Dan. 12:3).

Ask the Lord to help you witness for Him.

What can senior adults do when dependent and helpless?

A preacher friend told me the most loved person in his large circle of kinfolk was a cousin almost completely helpless. Relatives took turns waiting on him. The cousin was so appreciative and loving that even the children enjoyed being with him and waiting on him. Although absolutely dependent on others, he greatly blessed them. The preacher said this helpless cousin with his appreciation and love sends everyone on their way feeling happy and worthwhile.

Helpless persons do not do much good by moaning and complaining about their condition. Certainly dependent persons must be aware of their condition and recognize their limitations. Let them realize though that they have something worth more than gold. Let them care greatly for others and show their appreciation and love.

Doing things for others is good. However, letting others do something good for you is as good as doing something for them. A hard thing to do is let someone help you. You can do more than you realize. Ask them what they do, what they like, where they go, and so forth. Listen to them and respond. Thank them for sharing with you. That will bless them and also give you something to think and pray about.

In His Sermon on the Mount Jesus said, "Let your light so shine before men, that they may see your good works, and glorify your Father which is in heaven" (Matt. 5:16).

Ask God to help you to let others do things for you and then to show them loving appreciation.

How should senior adults treat their children and grandchildren?

One of the most important things senior adults can do is to keep up good relationships with their children and grandchildren. We could make a long list of things we need to do about those relationships. The very best thing to do is to ask God to help us be good parents and grandparents.

A Prayer for Parents and Grandparents to Pray

Thank You, Lord, for being my loving Heavenly Father. Help me to treat my children and grandchildren as You treat me.

Help me to be interested in their hopes and desires, their needs and problems, and their thoughts and feelings. Make me a good listener and encourager.

Lead me that I might not be offensive in word or tone of voice. Help me not to be easily offended or embarrassed. Let me laugh with them in natural enjoyment and shed tears in mutual concern.

Guide me that I will not lose my patience, scold, or speak harshly. Help me to express concern in a tactful way and also to express honest praise and commendation.

Give me confidence in them and help me show it in what I say and do. Let me do good things for them without trying to make them dependent on me. Amen.

"If ye then, being evil, know how to give good gifts

unto your children, how much more shall your Father which is in heaven give good things to them that ask him?" (Matt. 7:11)

Ask God to help you to be a blessing to your children and grandchildren in such a way that they will thank and glorify God.

How does the faith of senior adults affect their lives?

Surveys seem to agree that over half of Americans, maybe as many as two thirds, are members of churches. Three fourths have some religious beliefs. However, only about one fourth think of themselves as very religious. Persons who feel they are very religious have religious beliefs that affect their views about family, morals, ethics, and so forth.

Those who take their faith seriously say they have had a religious experience, study the Bible, pray, and attend church.

Senior adults who are very religious report their faith benefits them.

1. They are certain about their salvation. They believe they are precious to God because He has saved them by Jesus Christ.

2. They are confident they are children of God. That means that their death will be a passage from earthly life to everlasting life with Christ in heaven.

3. They feel they are members of an extended family where all Christians are brothers and sisters in Christ.

4. They will have pleasant experiences and good fellowship by participating in the activities of their church.

Many Bible passages tell how to get much out of your

Christian commitment. Here is a favorite: "Fulfil ye my joy, that ye be likeminded, having the same love, being of one accord, of one mind. Let nothing be done through strife or vainglory; but in lowliness of mind let each esteem other better than themselves" (Phil 2:2-3).

Ask God to help you be the best Christian you can be.

Do your thoughts and feelings affect your health?

A man I knew would not take medicine because he said he trusted the Lord and to take medicine would show a lack of faith in God. That is one extreme. The other extreme is that a lot of people do not bother to pray because they are getting medical treatment.

Are these two approaches contrary to each other? Not really.

Taking medicine is like eating. It is taking physical matter into your body to help the body function properly. We pray before we eat. Why not pray also when we take medicine?

A highly specialized doctor said one's attitude was just as important as the medicine he prescribed. He said that a negative attitude could block the effectiveness of medical treatment. He was sure a body is sensitive to a person's feelings. It may also be sensitive to a person's thoughts.

A lot of publicity has been given to the story of a well-known man who, according to his doctor, had only a year to live. He was convinced that laughter would help him get well. He got a bunch of old funny movies and laughed and laughed. He laughed himself—not to death—but back to health.

When you are ill, why not take your medicine, think about good things, and generate pleasant feelings?

Just as you eat the food God has given human beings to cultivate and prepare, take the medicine He has given us to cope with diseases and pain.

Even in ancient times the Bible emphasized the importance of medicine and a person's feelings: "A merry heart doeth good like a medicine: but a broken spirit drieth the bones" (Prov. 17:22).

Ask God to help you have both physical and spiritual health.

What help can senior adults be to their pastor?
As senior adults we can follow the leadership of the pastor. We can also actively encourage him.

Many people expect a new pastor to be perfect the day he arrives, but they also expect him to improve further. Accept your pastor as a human being who has strengths and weaknesses which are different from any other pastor.

Get acquainted with him. A step in that direction is to have him and his family into your home or take them out to dinner. Remember his children so that you can call their names when you see them next.

Help him to get acquainted with others. If you are a teacher, director, or committee chairman, invite the pastor to meet with your group to make a brief statement about his support for it and what he would like to see it do. If you are not one of these leaders, suggest to the leader that it might be done.

Find out what help he would like from you. Would he like for you to let him know about sick people and about other matters? Are there things you could volunteer to do?

Jesus said about those He sent out to minister, "The

workman is worthy of his meat" (Matt. 10:10).

Ask God to help you support your pastor spiritually and emotionally as well as physically.

What can senior adults do for their church?

In many churches senior adults make up a higher percentage of the membership than the percentage of senior adults in the neighborhood population. Senior adults can help their church in a variety of ways. As a senior adult, you can help your church by attending it regularly, keeping informed about its work, supporting it financially, and praying for it. You have, no doubt, already thought about those ways of helping and they are good.

My wife offered some practical suggestions I might not have thought of.

Senior adults are good at fixing cookies, cupcakes, and so forth, for activities of children and youth. You might offer to do this on a limited basis, say once a week, once a month, or once a quarter.

Senior adults could upgrade their own meeting place in the church with painting, blinds, floor covering, and so forth. Both men and women could help.

You could also help upgrade rooms and facilities of other age groups.

Invite the pastor or other church leaders to senior-adult classes, departments, or activities as guests or speakers.

A Bible verse we teach children would be good for us senior adults also: "Be ye kind one to another" (Eph. 4:32).

Ask God to help you do things for your fellow church members.

Should senior adults have a daily schedule?

Routine can get monotonous unless it is built on the needs and rhythm of life. Try this:

Daily Dozen for Senior Adults

1. Arise and shine. Waking up is an art. First, thank God for the night's rest and tell Him you love Him. Stretch and get up.

2. Take care of your physical needs. Wash and do the things you need to do every morning.

3. Eat what is good for you. Realize that what you eat is important to your health and feelings.

4. Take time to read the Bible and rejoice in God's presence.

5. Plan interesting things for the day and the days to come.

6. Exercise. Even a person confined to bed needs exercise.

7. Do something for others. At least think of them.

8. Learn something. Do this by reading, by watching TV, or by talking to someone. At the day's end think of what you learned.

9. Get out of your house, your room, your chair—if you can.

10. Love people. Think of persons and how much you appreciate them. Then pray for them.

11. Rest. Resting as you need it is like rhythm in music.

12. Enjoy yourself. Laugh at something every day. Smile a lot also.

You cannot count on tomorrow and so make the most of today. "Do not boast about tomorrow, for you do not know what a day may bring forth" (Prov. 27:1, NIV).

Ask God each day to guide you for twenty-four hours.

7.

I Need Thee Every Hour

Senior adults need help.

In 1934 a California man named Townsend proposed that persons over sixty receive $200 a month from the federal government. In 1934, $200 was more than some working people made.

The Townsend Plan didn't make it, but a year later in 1935 Congress passed the Social Security Act. There are senior adults alive and comfortable today because of what Congress did then.

Some senior adults could not survive or have medical care without the help of Social Security. Even with that some people need more, and some states also have plans that help senior adults.

What do senior adults need? They need what all other adults need. They need to survive, be comfortable, and be sure about what is coming. Furthermore, they need to care for people and feel that people care for them. They also need to be a vital part of something worthwhile that has meaning beyond them. In addition, they need to experience ongoing fulfillment. Within each of these needs and beyond them is the need for senior adults to feel good about their individual selves.

Senior adults who have worked hard all their lives to meet their own needs will continue to do so in their advanced years. However, any of us may need help at some particular point Senior adults will find help when they need it if they are members of a caring group.

Churches with their commitment to trusting, hoping, and caring are helpful in meeting the needs of senior adults. Churches have a variety of resources ranging from places to meet, good literature, helpful counsel, individual assistance, activities, and opportunities for senior adults themselves to do worthwhile things.

Some churches concentrate on the needs of senior adults who are church members. Many churches seek to reach out to senior adults beyond their own members. Churches would do well to plan what services or help they would like to offer perhaps as an outreach ministry in their neighborhood or larger community.

Any senior adults would find great help from the regular efforts and activities of a church, especially if someone had the responsibility to meet and greet them should they visit the church. Senior adults need to meet people who are trusting and trustworthy, who are optimistic and pleasant, and who are loving and lovable.

A church offers more to senior adults than do most organizations that are just for senior adults. Older people who attend a church have contact with younger adults, youth, and children. This wider association will benefit not only senior adults but also the younger groups of persons.

Few churches can provide all of the help senior

adults need. Therefore most of them will need to learn what help is available elsewhere and how persons who need it can get that additional help.

How can senior adults get the help they need?

You may think the answer to this question is so obvious that it doesn't need attention. However, some people need to consider this question and the answer. I am one of those persons. However, not all persons who need this question answered are like I am.

My problem is that I am insensitive, stubborn, proud, and self-sufficient. Some of you are like that and maybe worse.

First, in order to get help, recognize your needs. A psychologist examining me for a job told me that I was insensitive to my own needs. He quickly said, "Don't grin so smugly. It isn't good. You are a danger to yourself. You don't know you have needs and, if you do realize it, you ignore them. You are self-sufficient and proud of it. Wise up! Recognize your needs and do something about them." That was good advice.

Second, do something about your needs. You may be able to take care of them yourself or you may get advice from a family member or friend. Get whatever help you need.

Third, follow through on what needs to be done. Treat your body, mind, and spirit as gifts from God and be a good steward of your fitness in all areas.

Fourth, with your needs met, apply yourself better to the things that will benefit you, that will bless others, and that will glorify God.

"Let us therefore come boldly unto the throne of grace, that we may obtain mercy, and find grace to help in time of need" (Heb. 4:16).

Ask God to supply your needs according to His riches in glory.

What can senior adults do about prolonged depressed feelings?

Soon after I received the doctor of theology degree, our seven-year-old son and his pal stood in front of our house yelling, "Dr. Gray! Dr. Gray!" Opening the door, I scowled and said, "What do you want?" They snickered and moaned in unison, "We're sick." Irritated by their humor, I gruffly commanded, "Then go to your rooms and go to bed!" My wife had come up behind me and she whispered, "Don't make them do that." So I chuckled at them and they jumped up and down as they laughed loudly.

My doctorate in theology doesn't qualify me to practice medicine, but I can give you good advice.

Depressed feelings range from being sad and lonely to such depression that it could be a serious health problem. Are you inclined to feel blue and be sorry for yourself? It may be nothing but "cabin fever." You may simply need to get out into the sunshine, enjoy the outdoors, talk to someone and laugh, hug and be hugged.

However, depression can be such that you need professional help. Start with your doctor and do what he says. If you do not improve, ask him to make an appointment for you with a specialist.

Depression is more serious than people realize. Do something about it.

As you take steps to improve your depressed feelings, seek the Lord's help. Join the psalmist in saying,

"Unto thee, O Lord, do I lift up my soul" (Ps. 25:1).

Pray for the Lord's guidance in doing what you should.

What can senior adults do about feeling blue?

This is like asking what causes a person to feel sick.

Depressed feelings can come from a physical disorder or from mental and emotional problems. This is why a person with continuing depression needs to see a physician.

On the other hand feeling blue or low in spirit may come from anger, stress, or fear. It can be a minor thing.

Anger is hard on you. It is one of the strong, basic emotions that can be both helpful and harmful. Anger that energizes you to action and helps resolve the irritant cause may be helpful. If it does not help you solve the problem, anger can damage you and thrust you into a spirit of depression. Fear and distress can also plunge your feelings to a low.

Think through what is causing your blues. Recognizing the problem can help.

Be good to yourself. You may need to give yourself some rest by getting a good night's sleep and even taking some extra rest. Buying yourself something or doing something you have wanted to do can also give you a boost.

Deliberately think good thoughts. Read your favorite passage of the Bible: Psalms, Proverbs, or the Sermon on the Mount (Matt. 5—7). Philippians 4:6-19 is also a good biblical antidepressant. Sing cheerful songs, especially some Christian hymns and choruses. Pray for God's help.

Thank God for specific blessings, praising Him, and asking Him to help you do something good for someone. Ask Him to lift up your feelings and to give you inner peace and joy.

What can a senior adult do about self-pity?

Do you feel like the person who said, "If it weren't for self-pity, I wouldn't be getting any pity at all"? Another person said, "I'm having a pity party and nobody but me came."

Do you feel blue often, like nobody cares about you and a lot of things have gone wrong? Do you get down in your spirit without any desire to do things?

Don't get in the habit of enjoying self-pity. That can become a way of life with senior adults. Feeling sorry for yourself can happen to you before you realize it. Anybody can get "down in the dumps." Without realizing it a person can sink into self-pity because it may attract attention and win some concern. Don't let feeling blue become a daily pastime.

Do something about your depressed feeling. Seek to identify the cause, especially if the cause is a negative emotion. Then you may be able to do something to counteract the bad effect of your negative feelings. Sleep and good nourishment can also help. Talking about the matter ventilates the problem and may blow self-pity away. Improve your feelings through devotional reading of the Bible, listening to or singing happy music, fellowshipping with Christian friends, thinking of good times, and counting your blessings.

Take charge of yourself and do as David in these words: "Bless the Lord, O my soul: and all that is within me, bless his holy name" (Ps. 103:1).

Pray to the Lord about your problem and ask His help.

What can a church do for senior adults?

Early Christians took care of their senior adults. Note Paul's instructions to Timothy (1 Tim. 5:1-10). He began by telling him not to scold an older man: "Rebuke not an elder" (v. 1). "Elder" is used in verse 17 for church officers but in verse 1 Paul seems to have meant an aged man. Later he mentioned taking care of widows and referred especially to those over sixty (v. 9).

A church can do several things for senior adults:

1. Keep up with them. Maintain their names on the roll and make sure someone is responsible for every senior adult. One senior adult can be responsible for another senior adult. Have someone call homebound senior adults every day.

2. Provide senior adults with good Christian literature, particularly Sunday School material and senior adult publications.

3. Arrange transportation to church, to doctor's offices, to shop, and so forth.

4. Offer conferences on health, hobbies, housing (rest homes and other), making wills, funeral plans, and so forth.

5. Plan special activities such as trips, fellowship meetings, joint activities with senior adults from other areas, and so forth.

6. Use senior adults. Recognize them; organize them to help as they can (some churches use them as money-counters); have a senior-adult singing group; and so forth.

Pray for God's guidance in ministering to senior adults.

Does a person show a lack of faith in God by taking medicine?

My dad was a boy in the 1880s and he told me about a doctor then who had a jug of cure-all medicine. The gossip was that the doctor dumped bits of medicine he had left in the jug along with some whiskey. When he didn't know what to give people, he would give them a bottle of the "cure-all" and prescribe three spoons a day. He said it worked because of those who took it more lived than died.

The idea that taking medicine shows a lack of trust in God goes back further than that even. Nothing in the Bible condemns good health care or the taking of medicine.

The Old Testament speaks well of medicine: "A merry heart doeth good like a medicine" (Prov. 17:22). A prophet had a vision of a stream with trees whose fruit would be good to eat and whose leaves would be medicine or for healing (Ezek. 47:12).

Jesus Himself said, "They are that whole have no need of the physician, but they that are sick" (Mark 2:17). With these words Jesus taught that sinners needed the salvation He offered just as sick people needed the help of a doctor.

Paul referred to a cherished associate as "Luke, the beloved physician" (Col. 4:14).

Once medicine was a healing art and varied greatly with each practitioner. Now it is a science of healing and much more precise and trustworthy. Of course, we should not let medicine or food or any other physical blessing blind us to the divine Giver.

Ask God to help you take good care of yourself.

Why do senior adults give so much to television preachers?

About 1930 when money was hard to come by, I saw a man throw money into the street for boys to scramble after and fight over. He was a vile man and expressed his vileness in an indecent way.

What people do with their money tells a lot about them.

Some senior adults give generously to television programs. I think they do that because of the good they receive and because of the good they want to do by their giving.

I am not defending nor judging them. I am trying to understand them. They are lonely and loving people who respond to a voice or program that speaks to them about the Lord. They are grateful for that and want that ministry to continue. In addition, the voice assures them that what they send is desperately needed and will do great good.

Senior adults need a ministry like this and it needs to be trustworthy. One church has a tape ministry to a dozen shut-ins. The Sunday morning service is recorded, duplicated on tapes Sunday afternoon, distributed Sunday night to volunteers who deliver a tape to a shut-in during the week and pick up the previous week's tape. To begin this ministry the church supplied a small tape player to each shut-in. The plan works well.

Take the Great Commission (Matt. 28:18-20) seriously. You don't have to go to a foreign country; you can start obeying it as you step out of your church door.

Ask God to help your church minister to senior adults and also to everyone else.

What would be good programs for a senior-adult group?

Many senior-adult groups meet regularly. Some have a program regularly, and some have informal social times. You might want to have a speaker or conference leader occasionally.

All senior adults have physical needs. A doctor who has some knowledge of the physical problems of aging might donate his time leading a conference as a community service.

Many senior adults need financial advice about investment, budgeting, and writing wills. You might find a resource person in your church, your bank, or your denomination's state office.

Senior adults experience many changes upon retirement and they keep on facing changes, some they had not anticipated. A good resource person would be a government worker with senior adults, a college professor in psychology or sociology, or a student studying in one of those areas.

Many senior adults lose contact with other people and come to feel alone and rejected. Someone in your group might lead in a discussion of this problem and make plans to seek to help persons who have become isolated.

A lot of senior adults feel they have lost standing or status. A neighboring pastor or your own pastor might be a good resource to help your group consider this problem.

The Bible encourages us to seek answers: "Happy is the man that findeth wisdom" (Prov. 3:13).

Ask God to guide you and others in finding help.

What needs can an organized senior-adult group meet?

An organized group of senior adults needs to do more than just meet and eat. Getting together and eating are good things to do but people have needs that can be met only by careful planning. Consider the different needs that programs and activities might meet.

1. Help individuals to feel someone knows who they are and what they are like as persons.

2. Give persons a sense of belonging to an ongoing, worthwhile group.

3. Provide an opportunity for senior adults to get acquainted and to care for each other.

4. Make persons more aware of how to take good care of themselves, physically, mentally, and emotionally.

5. Give opportunities for senior adults to express themselves in their own unique ways in productive activities.

6. Expose persons to new experiences and new interests.

7. Enable senior adults to take part in helping persons or society in general beyond their usual activities.

Such activities can add to a person's years and quality of life.

The Bible itself expresses a concern about the needs of older persons: "That the aged men be sober, grave, temperate, sound in faith, in charity, in patience. The aged women likewise, that they be in behaviour as becometh holiness" (Titus 2:2-3).

Ask God to bless senior organizations in their activities.

Why do people quit visiting senior adult shut-ins?

I changed this question slightly. The original question was "Why do pastors quit visiting senior adults?" I changed the wording because I am sure pastors are not the only ones who fail to visit senior adults.

A church where I was pastor had eight senior adult shut-ins and the complaint came that I was not visiting them enough. I knew that was true. I had unintentionally neglected them because I was busy, had other high priority visits to make, and so forth. On a small card I wrote their names, put the card in my pocket, and wrote the date of each call by the name. Soon I had eight senior adults assuring me of their love and promising to pray for me as I preached every Sunday morning.

People are busy and, unless they schedule themselves, they will fail to do what they ought to do and want to do.

Now, let me give shut-ins a few tips:

1. Think of yourself as being worth a visit. Appreciate and love those who visit you and the visit will be worth their time.

2. Share with them your joys and hopes as well as needs. Also show an interest in the one visiting you. Ask them to pray for you and promise to pray for them at some specific time.

3. Have confidence in yourself that you will be such

a blessing to them that they will look forward to seeing you again.

For those who visit shut-ins: "Forsake me not when my strength faileth" (Ps. 71:9).

Ask the Lord to bless those who visit shut-ins.

8.

Make Me a Blessing

Senior adults find meaning in their relations with others.

Years ago somebody I thought was a smart aleck said, "It isn't what you know; it's who you know that counts." Whoever first said that to me said it with a laughing sneer. The idea was that you did not have to know much if you had a "pull" with somebody who had influence.

That saying promotes a bad idea. A person's knowledge and skill should be worth a lot to himself and others. Even though I don't like the saying, it is true if you do not think of it as referring to improper influence in securing a job.

I greatly appreciate knowledge, wisdom, and skills. However I have learned that those personal qualities are low on life's scale of values compared to good relations with people.

Your love for people and their love for you are more important than scholastic degrees, worldly honors, or even wealth. People may become more aware of the value of good relationships as they become senior adults.

Some senior adults are miserable and they do not realize that it is because of their poor relationships with people.

Relationships begin with those immediately next to you and then expand outward like the concentric circles made when you pitch a rock into a pond. Think about that pattern: it moves from the center outward. That is how relationships work. They start with you. The better relationships you have with those closest to you, the better your relationships will be with others.

Some people are like my Granddad McCoy. He fussed all the time with his sons and daughters, less with his grandchildren, only a little with nephews and nieces, hardly any with neighbors, and he got along well with strangers.

I am a lot like my granddad and brag about him. However I work hard to be the kind of person I think he could have been if he had been loving and gentle to his family.

Relating to people or loving them is a skill like driving nails or baking a cake. You can do it well or you can do it poorly. However, you cannot relate well to people if you do not learn how and work at it.

At any age you can improve on the skill of relating to people. I will admit that it is possible to relate fairly well to people without loving them. Without love though, what seems to be good relationship may be only skillful and selfish manipulation.

Let us senior adults work on growing in our love for people. To love others is not to exploit them and rule over them. To love is to look for the good in others, to rejoice in their accomplishments, to encourage and reinforce them, to do anything you can for their good, to pray for God to bless them and draw them close to Him, and to enjoy being with them. When you love someone in that way, seek to extend that love outward to others.

Is it worth the trouble for me to go to church on Sunday?

Getting ready to go to church and getting there can be a big problem for senior adults. I assure you it is worth your trouble.

Christians need to meet together. The Bible says,

> Let us consider one another to provoke unto love and to good works: Not forsaking the assembling of ourselves together, as the manner of some is; but exhorting one another: and so much the more, as ye see the day approaching (Heb. 10:24-25).

Meeting with other Christians is a good relationship for you in several ways:

1. Jesus said we could experience His presence by meeting together: "Where two or three are gathered together in my name, there am I in the midst of them" (Matt. 18:20).

2. We need to meet together for the same reason the early Christians did. They met to study Christian teachings, to share with each other, to break bread together, and to pray (Acts 2:42). They were blessed by divine awe coming upon them and by seeing wonderful things happen. The Bible describes that experience as follows: "Fear came upon every soul: and many wonders and signs were done by the apostles" (v. 43). You could miss something great by not meeting with your fellow Christians.

3. Furthermore you can be a blessing to others by

meeting with them for prayers. "Confess your faults to one another, and pray for one another, that ye may be healed. The effectual fervent prayer of a righteous man availeth much" (Jas. 5:16).

Ask God to bless His people as they meet together.

What about a senior adults couple living together unmarried?

Some senior adults live together as husband and wife without marrying. One reason for this is that certain regulations let two people have more to live on if they live together as two single persons rather than as a married couple. A man and woman living together without being married are treated as two single persons. Such a regulation actually pays a man and woman to live together without marrying.

Some people actually ask, "What harm is there for an older couple to live together unwed if it helps them financially?" The harm would be to their own peace of mind, to the example set for younger persons, to the commitment to the divine plan for sexual relations, and to society's need to protect people in any contractual relation.

Any individual has society's protection up to a point. Living together involves rights and responsibilities. By licensing a marriage, society recognizes marriage's benefits and obligations and guarantees society's protection of each individual.

Marriage involves one's conscience, respect from others, the order of society, and God's approval. The Bible confirms marriage as both a social and a sacred relationship. Note the first couple (Gen. 2:18-25), the Seventh Commandment (Ex. 20:14), Jesus at the wedding in Cana (John 2:1-11), and Paul's teaching (Eph. 5:22-33). "For this cause shall a man leave his father and mother, and shall be joined unto his wife, and they two shall be one flesh" (Eph. 5:31).

Ask God to help you make your home what He wants it to be.

What can one do for a spouse, in a terminal condition?

How hard it is to undergo a spouse's decline with terminal illness. People who pray for someone who is dying will often ask the Lord to strengthen and comfort the surviving spouse.

Memory of the good times together may help you to bear the sadness and despair.

Your faith can also help. Trust God. When people greatly need the Lord, He will be close to them. Be open and honest with Him. You can say things to Him that you could not say to anyone else. Remember how frank Job was to God.

Patience will help you bear your burden and it will also contribute to your spiritual growth. Impatience will not help you, and can even destroy your health.

Reading the Bible also helps. Read Psalm 23 again and again. The Lord is indeed your shepherd, and He will take as good care of you as a good shepherd does of his sheep (v. 1). He will walk with you all of the way through the valley of the shadow of death and His presence with you will give you the strength to overcome fear (v. 4).

Taking care of a dying loved one is one of the hardest things in the world. As you go through it, this difficult experience can have an amazing blessing if you trust yourself completely to God.

Jesus gave an invitation you can take personally: "Come unto me, all ye that labour and are heavy laden, and I will give you rest" (Matt. 11:28).

Ask God for strength, wisdom, and love.

What should aging parents and their children do for each other?

I remember twenty years ago when I was in my fifties, our older son gently offered me some advice about something he thought I ought to do. I had a mixture of feelings. I was a little shocked, a little bit amused, and very pleased.

Families differ so much that it is difficult to give general advice for the relationship between parents and their adult children. The earlier relationship between parents and their children during their childhood and youth affect the relationship in the later years. For instance, in some families the struggle for control in the children's adolescent years turns into a fierce battle in the children's adult years.

Senior adults and their adult children will have to work together at having a good relationship. That relationship will change through the years as each person's situation changes.

In one of his letters Paul compared his relationship to a church to the relationship of parents to their children: "I will not be a burden to you, because what I want is not your possessions but you. After all, children should not have to save up for their parents, but parents for their children" (2 Cor. 12:14 ,NIV).

A good relationship grows out of people's needs for each other rather than their need for each other's possessions. Love each other enough that you will do good things for the other and let the other do good things for you.

Ask the Lord to help you in your relationships with your family.

Should senior adults live near their children?

My mother lived with us for awhile and then got her own apartment. She lived in the same town, even making moves when we did. We visited her at least once a week, brought her to our house every two or three weeks, and called her often. It was almost an ideal situation. When we moved out of the state, she moved to be near my sister. That situation worked well but it does not always do so.

Senior adults need to be near people they care for. Because of friends and long-established relationships, many senior adults stay where they had lived for years. However, many move to "villages" or neighborhoods built especially for them.

Really, no single answer to this question will satisfy all senior adults. Parents and children need to consider all options. The parents need to think about what they will give up and also what they will gain. The children also must think about what is involved from their standpoint.

The Bible establishes the obligation that parents and children have for each other, but it does not tell how that obligation should be fulfilled. "If any provide not for his own, and specially for those of his own house, he hath denied the faith, and is worse than an infidel" (1 Tim. 5:8). Since the Lord expects parents and children to help each other, you can call on Him for guidance in your own situation.

Ask God to help you be a blessing to your own family members.

Why do I feel guilty about putting my parent in a care center?

Tears came as a woman told of taking her mother to a center where the eighty-year-old mother could have full care and available emergency attention aroundthe clock. She said, "I know it is the only thing to do, but I do not feel good about it."

The daughter was willing to wear her own self out and to sacrifice her health taking care of her mother. However, she and the rest of the family knew that was not the best thing for the aging mother nor for anyone else.

Should you listen to your feelings or be guided by reason? Here is where love can guide you if it is more than impulsive emotion. This is the *agape* love of the New Testament. Such love is more than just sentimental feeling. This kind of love *(agape)* is described in 1 Corinthians 13. With such love you deliberately care for someone so much you will do anything you can for that person's good. Rational love does not replace impulsive love. These two dimensions (or kinds) of love together form a love that can last. Rational love gives emotional love direction and endurance. Emotional love can give rational love power and joy. Put them together and you can do what is best for someone even when that is hard.

"Love is patient, love is kind. . . . It always protects, always trusts, always hopes, always perseveres. Love never fails" (1 Cor. 13:4,7-8, NIV).

Ask the Lord to help you love others so much you will do what you can for their good.

What can I do about conflict with younger family members?

Grandad McCoy, my mother's father, and I had an awful argument while I was a high-school senior. It was over Franklin D. Roosevelt. Our history teacher made us keep up with what FDR was doing and where he seemed to be leading. I thought I was a political expert and tried to explain to my granddad what Roosevelt was doing. Granddad didn't like FDR and tried to tell me what was wrong with Roosevelt and his politics. Our voices got louder until my mother called me out of the room. She said, "Stop fussing with your granddad! Don't ever argue with him again!"

I never fussed with him again. We got along well from then on. I worked at it and so did he, more than I realized. Three years later he loaned me forty dollars to buy my first car, a 1929 Model-A Ford.

Is there conflict between you and younger members of your family or between you and younger persons in general? If there is, work on the situation. Identify the differences in opinions and feelings between you. Recognize you can't make them be like you were as a youth or like you are now. You don't have to agree with them. Just love them.

Look for the good in them. Commend them for whatever good you see in them. Sympathize with them in their problems and encourage them. The Bible speaks of the good in both the young and old: "The glory of young men is their strength, gray hair [wisdom] the splendor of the old" (Prov. 20:29, NIV).

Ask God to protect, guide, and bless the younger generations.

What can senior adults and youth do for each other?

The pastor of a church realized the senior adults and youth were critical of each other. The senior adult department gave more than any other group in the church and the youth had the largest budget allocation of any group. Somebody needed to do more than just explain the different economic situations of the two age groups and help them appreciate each other.

The pastor and the youth workers set up a plan for the teenagers and also the children to adopt a senior adult to hug and to speak to every Sunday at church. Homebound senior adults were included in the plan and two youth or two young adults would adopt two homebound senior adults and call them every week and go see them at least once a month.

The pastor did not tell me what the senior adults did in return but they might have tried doing these things:

1. Learn and remember the names of the youth or children who adopted them. Write their names so they could remember them.

2. Get acquainted with those who adopted them.

3. Don't give individual gifts to their adopters. Some might not receive gifts from their adoptees and that could cause them to feel neglected.

4. If senior adults want to give gifts, put their money together and get Bibles, T-shirts, or other good items for all of the youth and children in the church.

5. Pray for their adopters regularly.

Ask God to bless the younger people in the church.

How can an aging couple get the most out of their marriage?

A woman described retirement as a time of less money and more husband. Sure enough, that's retirement! My wife and I are with each other a lot more. That is both good and bad. We snap at each other and bicker more, I think. On the other hand, we express our love more also.

Your relationship to God flavors everything else. This includes going to church together; prayer at the table; discussing church activities, God's will in decisions, concern for others, the Sunday School lesson; and sharing your awareness of God's will.

The relationship between the two of you is more important than ever because you are together so much. Being together more, we discuss future plans and finances more. We approach ideas tentatively so we can change our minds. We talk a lot, but we are comfortable not saying anything for hours unless our silence is hostile action; and sometimes it is, but we have learned to make up more quickly.

As a senior couple, find things to enjoy every day. That's the way to live—celebrate life together.

If husbands and wives will act like Christians, they will get along fine. Couples need to read Peter's advice to them (1 Pet. 3:1-7) and then his advice to Christians in the next two verses. He said that Christians should be harmonious, sympathetic, loving like a family, humble-minded, with no aim to get even or to hurt each other (vv.8-9).

Ask God to help you to treat each other like Christians.

What can a senior adults do about a spouse's faults?

At a senior-adult meeting a woman who was a new member met an older woman and they began to get acquainted. The younger woman's husband had just retired. They laughed at each others' jokes and then began to talk about problems of aging.

The new member said, "Our worst problem is my husband's snoring." The older woman answered, "I can sympathize. My husband used to snore."

The younger woman laughed, "What did you do?" Her new friend answered, "Nothing. He died three months ago."

They embraced and the younger whispered, "Thank you."

Seek to maintain and improve the quality of your relationship. If you can agree to talk about problems, that is good. Peace between a couple is worth almost anything, but peace is not peace if resentment festers within one partner of the marriage.

If you can, talk about it. Be brief, specific, and gentle. Do not be unkind nor lay down ultimatums. If you are the one with the fault, try to understand your spouse's view, and seek a solution. The right approach and the right response can make your marriage even sweeter.

Paul summed up his advice to couples like this: "Each one of you also must love his wife as he loves himself, and the wife must respect her husband" (Eph. 5:33, NIV). I think that also means, if a husband is to be loving and a wife respectful, then a wife must be lovable and a husband respectable.

Ask God to keep blessing your marriage.

What can senior adults do when a son or daughter dies?

The death of a son or daughter is hard to take. Our youngest son died when he was seven. After the funeral my wife said, "My arms ache; they are so empty." We held each other and wept.

A grown son of a family in our church died in a plane crash within sight of his parent's home. The father was bitter, but in time he found peace with God.

A comforting thought for bereaved parents is that God knows what it is for a son to die. My wife said to a bereaved mother, "I know what you are going through." The woman spoke harshly, "Oh, no you don't." When my wife told of her own loss, the two women embraced and wept together. God does know your sorrow and grief. Embrace Him in prayer and He will comfort you.

Others will comfort you too. Their prayers will help you.

Another comfort will be your hope. Heaven will mean more than ever to you when a beloved family member has gone on to that promised land.

Yet another comfort is to do something to honor the memory of the loved one who died. You could do something that would bless others for years. Some bereaved families designate a cause that friends may choose to contribute to as a memorial. Let this verse comfort you: "He being dead yet speaketh" (Heb. 11:4).

Ask God to strengthen and help you.

Do all senior adults need a will?

You have the right and even the responsibility to tell what you want done with what you have or might come to have after your death. You do that through a will.

What do you want done with what you have when you die? Write it all down. That is a will. You may be able to get help from somebody in your church. Some church groups have in their state offices persons who can help you make a will.

What should happen to your money and things when you die? The simplest answer to that question is that whatever you want is what should be done. Of course, you have a number of possibilities, such as your family, godly causes, or personal interests. and even your pet animals.

What can guide you in deciding what should be done with what you leave? Your will can do several things. It is a way to show your appreciation. You can also show what you care about. Then also your will can be a message and a guide to others.

This Old Testament prayer can give you guidance: "Now also when I am old and greyheaded, O God, forsake me not; until I have showed thy strength unto this generation, and thy power to every one that is to come" (Ps. 71:18).

Ask God for guidance in using what you have for the good of others and to His glory now and for all time to come.

How should I as a senior adult feel about myself?

As a youth I came across a poem that started like this:

"I have to live with myself,

and so I want to be fit for myself to know."

The book it was in listed the author as "Anonymous."

That poem was a challenge for youth then and it would be a good challenge for senior adults now. It spoke of being honest with yourself. Be able to look yourself straight in the eye and not hate yourself for what you had done. Respect yourself and also earn the respect of others. Be the kind of person that you yourself would like to meet.

You are the only one who knows the real you. Work hard at being the kind of a person you feel good about being. Be such that, no matter what happens, you will have a good conscience and you will respect yourself.

Our relationships with other people are determined largely by the way we feel about our own selves. For that reason the Bible says, "Thou shalt love thy neighbor as thyself" (Lev. 19:18; Mark 12:31).

In order to have the best relationship with God, you begin by recognizing that you are more like God than anything else in all of nature. You are a creature made in His image (Gen. 1:27). In addition to that, if you have received Jesus Christ as you Savior, you yourself are a child of God. That is not just a title; it is a personal reality. Let the truth of God's great love for you fill your whole being.

Ask God to help you see yourself as He wants you to.

9.

Going Home

Senior adults know their time on earth is getting shorter.

When I was in my fifties, a doctor told me to stop using caffeine. I said, "Do you mean coffee?" He answered, "I mean everything that has caffeine in it." Do you know that means tea, chocolate, cokes, many other soft drinks, and even some medicine?

I complained to my wife for years and finally declared that, if I were ever to get some disease that was terminal, I would take up drinking coffee again.

At sixty-five I realized that retirement was terminal. So, I began to drink a cup of coffee three times a week. I told my doctor and he said medical opinion had changed (as it sometimes does). He said, "Drink your coffee but not more than two cups a day."

I don't mean by my story about the coffee to imply that you should indulge in things that are wrong or harmful. No, Sir! I told you that in order to make the wisecrack about retirement being terminal. We senior adults have started the last mile of our life's journey on earth.

What I really mean to say is that, if you have been putting off doing things you want to do or should do, don't delay any longer. Go for it.

People's attitude toward death affects their whole life and that attitude greatly affects their senior years.

Death is the end of this earthly life. When you die, you cease to exist in this physical realm.

We Christians believe human life continues beyond physical death and that the relationship you establish in this life with God determines what kind of a life you will have hereafter. God Himself, through His Son, Jesus Christ, opens the door to full life after death to everyone who will take it. The marvelous thing about all of this is that God persists in treating human beings as free and responsible persons. He invites everyone to live forever with Him just as they lived on the earth. Anyone can make this choice. However, God forces no one to accept His invitation.

Death is a certainty. You have absolutely no choice about that. You cannot escape it. You may hasten it or delay it but you cannot prevent it. However, all persons do have a choice about the life they will have beyond their earthly death.

That choice must be made here in this world where you can see good and evil existing side by side. What will your choice be?

For the devil and humans who serve him, death is fiery torment, the bottomless pit, and the end of hope.

On the other hand some poets describe death as launching a ship, opening a door, entering a new land, and making a new beginning. That is what death is if you die in the Lord. What you do here about your relationship to God is final.

If God made us in His own image, why do we have to die?

An old proverb says, "Here today, gone tomorrow." That is true about many things, including life and death. Physical life ends in death. Physical death is normal. When a living thing dies, it ceases to function and the material of its body disperses into the environment around it. That is the physical side of death.

For people life is more than a physical reality. God formed people in His own image. It is true that human beings are physical but we are also spiritual because God breathed into us the life of the spirit. We are different from any other creature. Human beings are "living souls" (Gen. 2:7).

Humans face two deaths—a physical death and a spiritual death. Physical death is the end of your reliance on and use of physical matter. Spiritual death is separation from God in an everlasting hell. Physical death comes from illness and injuries. Spiritual death comes from sin. "The wages of sin is death" (Rom. 6:23). Sin is fatal to the human soul and it terminates forever the vital connection between a human being and God. Physical death separates one from earthly things. Spiritual death separates a person from godly things such as joy, peace, and love.

Physical death is essential because "flesh and blood cannot inherit the kingdom of God" (1 Cor. 15:50). Physical death is tragic for a person separated from God by sin since sin is "the sting of death" (1 Cor. 15:56).

Thank God for the victory He gives us through Jesus Christ (1 Cor. 15:57).

What can we do as we realize death is coming?

Surely everyone has heard this old saying: "Death is a certainty. The old must die and the young may." Medical science has done much to heal our diseases and to prolong life. However, as the years pass, you become more aware of death's approach. Some senior adults lose their dread of death and even begin to anticipate it.

The thing about dying is to be ready for it and for what comes after it. I am like the fellow who said, "I am ready to go anytime but I'm not in a hurry." People need to be serious about life and death. A father, concerned about his son who had no sense of responsibility said, "Son, if I died tomorrow, where would you be?" The son answered, "Why, I'd be here. The question, Dad, is, Where would you be?" We can joke about it but don't postpone answering the question of death and the hereafter.

What must you do in the face of death? Paul said, "Believe on the Lord Jesus Christ, and thou shalt be saved" (Acts 16:31).

If senior adults are assured of their own salvation, they need to do all they can to help those who will live on after them. Do your best to provide for them physically and spiritually. Help them to know of your faith in Christ and of your love for God. Be sure also that they are aware of your love for them, your appreciation for them and their good qualities, and your confidence that they will make the most of their lives.

Ask God to help you be faithful to Him both in living and in dying.

How can senior adults cope with the death of a spouse?

The death of a loved one brings you to one of life's most difficult experiences. Senior-adult couples know death can come anytime for either of them. Many accept this fact and make the most of their days realizing time is running out.

Coping with the death of a spouse begins even before the death occurs. Advance preparation for certain things can help. Some buy cemetery plots and make arrangements with a mortuary. You may plan together the program for the funeral or memorial service. Such advance preparation can ease some of the stress at the time of the death.

No two people grieve exactly alike but some things are typical. If you realize that your feelings during the grief period are natural, your grieving can help you rather than disturb you.

People differ in how much they depend on others but most find comfort when others join with them in grieving over the loss of a loved one. Getting back into your normal activities will help you regain your emotional balance. Plan for the days and years ahead.

Draw close to the Lord and be comforted by your assurance of heaven and the reunion we look forward to there. The Bible promises:

> Then we which are alive and remain shall be caught up together with them in the clouds to meet the Lord in the air: and so shall we ever be with the Lord. Wherefore comfort one another with these words (1 Thess. 4:17-18).

Ask the Lord to walk close to you and to comfort you.

Is cremation wrong?

Cremation is a funeral custom that goes back to ancient times. It is disposing of a dead body by fire. Our very word *funeral* comes from an ancient Sanskrit word meaning *smoke*. Vikings of Northern Europe, long before the discovery of America, practiced cremation by placing the dead body in a boat, setting the boat on fire, and pushing it out to sea.

Cremation is still used today as a form of burial. Those who favor cremation say that it is sanitary and economical, that it cuts down on the spread of disease, and that it saves land.

One problem, according to television murder mysteries, is that cremation creates trouble for police by destroying evidence needed to determine the cause of death.

Some oppose cremation because of their respect for the human body. Others wonder how there can be a bodily resurrection if the physical body is destroyed. Paul said flesh and blood cannot inherit the kingdom of God (1 Cor. 15:50). We shall have bodies but they will be like the resurrected body of Jesus. The Bible assures us that a preserved, physical corpse is not essential for a bodily resurrection: "The sea gave up the dead which were in it; and death and hell delivered up the dead which were in them" (Rev. 20:13). Paul taught, "This corruptible shall have put on incorruption, and this mortal shall have put on immortality" (1 Cor. 15:54). The Bible does not forbid cremation. Study 1 Corinthians 15:16-58.

Ask God to help you know what would be best for you, your family, and society, and what would glorify God most.

Can a person who commits suicide go to heaven?

A person who commits suicide will go to heaven if he has accepted Jesus Christ as Lord. First John 5:12 says, "He that hath the Son hath life."

The question is not whether suicide is a mortal sin which would separate a person from God eternally. The Bible teaches that salvation is everlasting life and that salvation is by grace. Ephesians 2:8 states: "By grace are ye saved through faith; and that not of yourselves: it is the gift of God."

Now, let's think about how bad suicide is. As bad as suicide is, something is worse. Refusing to believe that Jesus Christ is God's Son and refusing to accept Him as your Lord is worse than suicide, murder, or any other sin. Suicide is the murder of one's self and is tragic for someone who is not a Christian.

I have known persons I felt were Christians who committed suicide because of pain, loss of self-respect, and concern for family. Christians have no right to take their lives. How or when they die is not their choice. Of course, Christians have some choice about whether or not *to* sin. However, the sins of God's children do not separate them from their Heavenly Father. Sins offend God and add to the burden of Christ, but in His abounding grace God forgives all of our sins. That is no license to commit suicide or to sin. Paul said, "Shall we sin, because we are not under the law, but under grace? God forbid" (Rom. 6:15). A sinning Christian has Christ as his advocate with the Father (1 John 2:1).

Ask God to help you bless others and glorify the Lord.

What is euthanasia and is it wrong?

Euthanasia comes from two Greek words that literally mean *good death*. It means to kill persons painlessly for their own good. It is against the law in most of the world. Religious groups in general look on euthanasia either as suicide or murder. Therefore, they look on it as wrong.

Who would support euthanasia? Thoughtful, kind persons might. They say those suffering incurable, painful diseases should be able to have an injection that would end their suffering. The problem is: people have recovered from diseases diagnosed as incurable.

In our society human government is charged to protect and preserve life. If it is ever allowed to kill persons whose lives do not have quality or dignity, then all are in danger.

Another problem which is a practical one is whether euthanasia includes letting die a person who is being sustained solely by artificial means. (Look at the question after this one).

People in the medical profession have never before faced the moral questions they now confront often. Today's Christian theologians need to speak to the world about matters the great theologians of the past never dreamed of.

According to the Bible God is involved in every human life. "In whose [God's] hand is the soul of every living thing, and the breath of all mankind" (Job 12:10). "In him [God] we live, and move, and have our being" (Acts. 17:28).

Ask God to help us see His presence and power in all human life.

Should death be delayed by artificial life supports?

"When my life forces are failing and it is only a matter of time, don't keep me here with artificial means." That is what I have told my family.

Persons can make a "a living will." This is a legal document you can sign that will authorize the authorities not to prolong your life when you are dying. This relieves your survivors and the authorities of the responsibility for the decision.

Find out what the law is in your state. Check with your doctor, a hospital, or a senior adult group.

Being allowed to die naturally is not euthanasia. Defenders of a person's right to die without their death being needlessly prolonged speak of it as dying with dignity.

If you choose to make a living will, do it in agreement with you spouse and other members of the family. Your signature will need to be appropriately witnessed.

Related to this matter, some want to indicate the desire to donate their body organs for the use of other persons in need. In this way you might make it possible for someone else to live or perhaps to have eyesight.

We need not fear death nor resist it. Paul said, "For me to live is Christ, and to die is gain" (Phil. 1:21). Jesus said, "Be thou faithful unto death and I will give thee a crown of life" (Rev. 2:10).

Ask God to guide you in making decisions you need to make for the sake of others.

Should senior adults plan their funeral services in advance?

A worker with senior adults recommends that they plan their funeral services in advance. He says to do this in consultation with the other members of the family.

He points out that at the time of a person's death the surviving spouse or the surviving members of the family can be under stress both with grief and also from pressure of time to make the various arrangements within a few days. Because of this pressure of limited time, the more you can take care of in advance, the better.

Things you can take care of in advance include selection of a mortuary and purchase of a cemetery lot. You can put together important papers, such as insurance policy, mortgage and property deed, automobile papers, your will, and other legal documents.

Whether you plan your funeral in advance is up to you. If you do, keep in mind those who will probably attend it. In some funerals one or several persons make a brief personal comment about the deceased. You could indicate who these might be or set time in the service when volunteers could speak appreciation for the deceased. A person's pastor usually presides and delivers message of comfort.

The funeral should honor the deceased, comfort the survivors, and glorify the Lord.

Here is a Scripture verse to guide in planning a funeral: "Blessed are the dead which die in the Lord" (Rev. 14:13).

Pray that your funeral will comfort others and honor God.

10

In the Sweet By and By

The hope of senior adults for heaven blesses them.

I remember many experiences but the one that affected me most happened when I was nine years old. I accepted Jesus Christ as my Savior and Lord. I felt great relief and intense joy.

Trusting Christ for salvation is the basis for my hope of going to heaven.

Hope is more than wishing. For instance, people say, "I hope the sun will shine tomorrow." Most who say something like that are only expressing a wish. If hope is just wishing, it can be a dream fantasy and practically worthless.

In the Bible hope is on the same level as faith and love. Hope is looking forward so much to the good that is coming that it affects what you do now. We are inclined to think that the past determines the present. If that were true, then the present would be a continuation of what has been. Things would keep on being the same. Hope changes things.

Hope makes a difference because, when people look forward, they do something. When persons want something more than what they have, they make things happen. By hope Abraham left Ur. By hope the Israelites left Egypt. By hope people accept Christ as Savior and by hope they live to please God.

My hope which began when I trusted Christ for salvation developed within me like a growing plant. I did not cultivate it much for years. When, as an adult, I became a pastor, I cultivated hope enough to share it with others, especially those who were seriously ill. You might say my hope grew to be as tall as my mind. My hope became a mental concept, and I tried to explain it in comforting people and in preaching.

The time came when my hope had a sudden, massive growth. That was when our seven-year-old son died from an accident. Then my hope became a strong anticipation within me. It was no longer just a mental concept. It became part of my spiritual framework along with faith and love.

When senior adults look forward to the joys of heaven, that hope gives great quality to their lives. Hope grows out of faith but, if it is to grow very much, you need to work at developing it. Hope can grow if you will study the Bible, pray, enjoy fellowship with Christians, and walk daily with the Lord.

Christian hope assures you: "The coming of the Lord draweth nigh" (Jas. 5:8).

Jesus said, "If I go and prepare a place for you, I will come again, and receive you unto myself; that where I am, there ye may be also" (John 14:3).

Let your hope guide you in getting ready for His coming so that, when you stand before Him, He will not only acknowledge you as one of His followers but will also speak those wonderful words of commendation, "Well done" (Matt. 25:21).

What will our bodies be like in heaven?

I, too, would like to know the answer since I expect to occupy my resurrected body for all eternity.

The body we have in our earthly life is the material part of us. It has both substance and shape. Our body is an essential part of our being. We did not exist until we came into this world as a baby in bodily form. We continue to exist in this world as long as we have a physical body that functions. Our bodies help to form our personalities, and our personalities influence the appearance of our bodies. The physical body is so much a part of us that, when it suffers, we suffer.

The saved will rise from the dead with bodies which Paul described as immortal and incorruptible (1 Cor. 15:54). In that body or form we will not be subject to disease or death.

Paul referred indirectly to our resurrected bodies in these words: "If we have been planted together in the likeness of his death, we shall be also in the likeness of his resurrection" (Rom. 6:5) John said, "Now are we the sons of God, and it doth not yet appear what we shall be: but we know that, when he shall appear, we shall be like him; for we shall see him as he is" (1 John 3:2).

These verses indicate that the resurrected Jesus is the advance model of our future form. His disciples could see Him, recognize Him, touch Him. Jesus in His resurrected form could move, speak, and fellowship with His disciples.

Ask God to help you be what He wants you to be here and now.

When will the final judgment be and what will it be like?

The Bible speaks of judgment both as an ongoing action of God and also as a final action at the end of human life on earth. John the Baptist echoed the emphasis of earlier prophets on God's continuing judgment: "Now also the axe is laid unto the root of the trees: every tree therefore which bringeth not forth good fruit is hewn down, and cast into the fire" (Luke 3:9).

Jesus spoke of the final judgment,

> As the Father hath life in himself; so hath he given to the Son to have life in himself; and hath given to him authority to execute judgment also, because he is the Son of man. Marvel not at this: for the hour is coming, in the which all that are in the graves shall hear his voice, And shall come forth; they that have done good, unto the resurrection of life; and they that have done evil, unto the resurrection of damnation (John 5:26-29).

When a baby is born into this world, something begins that will never end. The only baby who existed before his earthly birth was Christ, the Son of God. Human beings are mortal. They will all die except those living at the time of Christ's return. In spite of the fact that they will die, every one of them will continue to exist forever. They shall appear before Christ for His final judgment of them. All have sinned and are already condemned. The issue in the final judgment will be to separate those who repented of their sins and trusted themselves to Christ from those who kept doing evil. See Matthew 25:31-46; Revelation 20:11-15.

Ask God to help you tell others about God's gift of salvation.

Is there anything to reincarnation?

A belief in reincarnation has reappeared in these days along with other ancient false beliefs such as witchcraft, astrology, and fortune-telling. Reincarnation is contrary to the Bible teaching of individual responsibility and final judgment.

Reincarnation is a belief in the transmigration of the soul. That is a form of animism, the religion of primitive people. They believed that every living thing, plant or animal, had a spirit and that at death a creature's spirit entered into the newborn body of some other living thing.

This false teaching appeared in ancient Egypt and Greece and became a part of Hinduism which taught that the process of soul transmigration continues until the spirit is purified and can then return to *nirvana*, its origin. The *karma* or character of the spirit in one life form determines the kind of life form it can inhabit next, whether animal or human, vicious or gentle. Buddha, who denied the existence of the soul, tolerated reincarnation because it had an explanation of why some suffered or prospered beyond what they deserved.

The Bible destroys the idea of reincarnation with this statement:

> Just as man is destined to die once, and after that to face judgment, so Christ was sacrificed once to take away the sins of many people; and he will appear a second time, not to bear sin, but to bring salvation to those who are waiting for him (Heb. 9:27-28, NIV).

Thank God for sending Christ to give us heavenly hope.

Will we know each other in heaven?

Two elderly preachers almost adopted me when I surrendered to preach.

One gave me over a hundred choice books.

The other didn't have much except a gentle spirit. I was eighteen, and he called me "Brother Gray," just as if I were a full-fledged preacher. Once when I visited him, we talked about heaven. His great hope made the experience a heavenly one for me. As he looked at me, huge tears slid down his cheeks and he said, "Soon I shall see my dear wife. Without that hope I would be miserable."

Yes, we shall know each other in heaven. Jesus specifically identified Abraham and Lazarus (Luke 17:19-23).

I like what W. T. Conner, a Southwestern Baptist Theological Seminary professor, said. Someone asked him if we would know each other in heaven. He answered, "Oh, I think we shall have as much sense over there as we have here."

Conner greatly stimulated my thinking about heaven. He said he thought we would be surprised to find heaven so much like our present existence on earth. Nobody asked him what he meant. It seemed clear when he said it. To me it meant that heaven and those in it would be as real to us as earth is now.

I anticipate heaven as a reunion. Paul said, "We know that the one who raised the Lord Jesus from the dead will also raise us with Jesus and present us with you in his presence" (2 Cor. 4:14, NIV).

Thank God for the hope of a heavenly reunion.

Will persons in heaven be sexless?

I thought a lot before including this question. If you don't want to read it, you have my permission to skip it.

No doubt this question grows out of the statement of Jesus: "In the resurrection they neither marry, nor are given in marriage but are as the angels of God in heaven" (Matt. 22:30).

This statement was in answer to the Sadducees who did not believe in the resurrection. They had used an absurd argument to support their denial of life after death. They told of a woman who had seven husbands during her life and asked whose wife she would be hereafter. Jesus said their question was irrelevant.

This question I am answering is also irrelevant.

The Sadducees thought in earthly terms and so do we. Here on earth we identify someone as to whether that person is a man or woman. We describe persons according to race, age, physical appearance, and other prominent physical items. Whether a person was fat or skinny will not be relevant in heaven.

If in heaven we are not known by sex, height, weight, age, and so forth, how shall we be identified? I don't know, but ignorance doesn't keep me quiet. Paul said that three things endure: "faith, hope and love" (1 Cor. 13:13, NIV). I wonder if we might be identified by how we measure out in those three enduring virtues. Maybe people will know us by the size, shape, and uniqueness of our love or of our faith or hope.

Ask God to help you grow in faith, hope, and love

since these could be very important in heaven.

What is the second coming of Christ and when will it happen?

During the rise of Hitler, Stalin, and Mussolini, many thought the time for Christ's return had come. I was a teenager then, and I was sure Christ's final coming would happen within my lifetime.

W. T. Conner said that Jesus identified His coming with the coming of the Kingdom: "There be some standing here, which shall not taste of death, till they see the Son of man coming in his kingdom" (Matt. 16:28). In that sense Christ comes all of the time. For instance, He returned after His resurrection and came to His disciples (John 16:16ff.). Then He came again when the Holy Spirit came at Pentecost. He keeps coming every time He saves someone and comes into that person's heart.

Conner also pointed out that Jesus spoke of a final coming (the second coming) which will be to end the earthly period of life and bring judgment on the world. When Jesus was on the earth, He Himself did not know when that final coming would be (Matt. 24:36).

In every period of history since Jesus lived on earth, His followers have lived in expectation of His "second coming." The continual anticipation of Christ's return has motivated Christians to great efforts of evangelism, missions, and ministry.

Many today think Christ will return before this decade ends. Let's realize it could happen, and intensify our efforts to reach people for Christ. Let's also realize that He may not come for another century. Therefore let's plan and carry out the greatest mission efforts the world has ever seen.

Pray for God's Kingdom to come.

What will the final judgment be like?

Judgment is a reality. It goes on all of the time. We constantly enjoy good results or suffer bad results because of our efforts. This should warn us that one's whole life with all its actions and extended influence will ultimately be judged.

Final judgment will occur when Christ returns.

> When the Son of man shall come in his glory, and all the holy angels with him, then shall he sit upon the throne of his glory: And before him shall be gathered all nations: and he shall separate them one from another, as a shepherd divideth his sheep from the goats (Matt. 25:31-32).

God will judge all people through Christ His Son. The purpose of judgment is not to discover human guilt but to reveal it for judgment. All will be found guilty and condemned.

God foresaw this plight of all human beings and He provided salvation through His Son Christ Jesus. Salvation is not automatic. God has respected the autonomy of the human soul and He protects its integrity. God offers salvation to all, but He does not force it on anyone.

People need to realize that the choice they make in life about their relationship to God is final, now and forever. God does not want anyone to perish and He has opened the door for all who will come to Him. Jesus said, "I am the door: by me if any man enter in, he shall be saved" (John 10:9).

Ask God to help you witness to people about the deliverance God has provided for them.

Is heaven as wonderful as they say?

One of the amazing things about heaven is that the Bible tells us so little about it. Surely that must be for our good. Of course, the Bible may tell us more than we realize.

I like what I find about heaven in Revelation 21 and 22. To begin with, heaven is presented as a new place (21:1) where tears will be wiped away and four things eliminated immediately—death, sorrow, crying, and pain (v. 4). The most obvious thing about heaven will be the presence and power of God and the Lamb (22:1). The life in heaven will be full and eternal (v. 2) and no evil will curse that life.

The statement, "his servants shall serve him," greatly excites me (v. 3). That sounds like we will have something productive to do. Maybe it will be geared to the spiritual qualities we develop in this life. That comment is pure speculation and you have just as much right to speculate about heaven within the Bible framework as I have.

We shall see Jesus there just as we see each other here. When others see us there, they can tell at a glance that we belong to Him (v. 4). We shall have light to see by but that light won't be from a blazing star nor from candles. The light will be God's own light which is Christ, our Lord (v. 5).

Heaven will last as long as God reigns and that will be forever and ever (v.5).

I'll look for you there!

Ask God to prepare you to serve Him in heaven.